Praise for *CSI*

"This book acutely 'follows the evidence' of *CSI*'s spectacle, setting, and seriality. Unusually for academic work, Derek Kompare also pays close attention to the show's developing characters. Careful, subtle, intelligent; Kompare takes *CSI* seriously not just as a brand, but as classic American television."

Matt Hills, Cardiff University

"Kompare shows that we should take *CSI* seriously as a dense and fascinating example of American popular culture which has appealed to millions of viewers over ten seasons and established itself as the most important network franchise of its time."

Roberta Pearson, University of Nottingham

Wiley-Blackwell Studies in Film and Television
Series Editors: Diane Negra and Yvonne Tasker

Experienced media studies teachers know that real breakthroughs in the classroom are often triggered by texts that an austere notion of the canon would disqualify. Unlike other short book series, **Wiley-Blackwell Studies in Film and Television** works from a broad field of prospective film and television programs, selected less for their adherence to definitions of "art" than for their resonance with audiences. From *Top Hat* to *Hairspray*, from early sitcoms to contemporary forensic dramas, the series encompasses a range of film and television material that reflects diverse genres, forms, styles, and periods. The texts explored here are known and recognized worldwide for their ability to generate discussion and debate about evolving media industries as well as, crucially, representations and conceptualizations of gender, class, citizenship, race, consumerism, and capitalism, and other facets of identity and experience. This series is designed to communicate these themes clearly and effectively to media studies students at all levels while also introducing groundbreaking scholarship of the very highest caliber. These are the films and shows we really want to watch, the new "teachable canon" of alternative classics that range from silent film to *CSI*.

CSI
DEREK KOMPARE

WILEY-BLACKWELL
A John Wiley & Sons, Ltd., Publication

This edition first published 2010
© 2010 Derek Kompare

Blackwell Publishing was acquired by John Wiley & Sons in February 2007. Blackwell's publishing program has been merged with Wiley's global Scientific, Technical, and Medical business to form Wiley-Blackwell.

Registered Office
John Wiley & Sons Ltd, The Atrium, Southern Gate, Chichester, West Sussex, PO19 8SQ, United Kingdom

Editorial Offices
350 Main Street, Malden, MA 02148-5020, USA
9600 Garsington Road, Oxford, OX4 2DQ, UK
The Atrium, Southern Gate, Chichester, West Sussex, PO19 8SQ, UK

For details of our global editorial offices, for customer services, and for information about how to apply for permission to reuse the copyright material in this book please see our website at www.wiley.com/wiley-blackwell.

The right of Derek Kompare to be identified as the author of this work has been asserted in accordance with the UK Copyright, Designs and Patents Act 1988.

All rights reserved. No part of this publication may be reproduced, stored in a retrieval system, or transmitted, in any form or by any means, electronic, mechanical, photocopying, recording or otherwise, except as permitted by the UK Copyright, Designs and Patents Act 1988, without the prior permission of the publisher.

Wiley also publishes its books in a variety of electronic formats. Some content that appears in print may not be available in electronic books.

Designations used by companies to distinguish their products are often claimed as trademarks. All brand names and product names used in this book are trade names, service marks, trademarks or registered trademarks of their respective owners. The publisher is not associated with any product or vendor mentioned in this book. This publication is designed to provide accurate and authoritative information in regard to the subject matter covered. It is sold on the understanding that the publisher is not engaged in rendering professional services. If professional advice or other expert assistance is required, the services of a competent professional should be sought.

Library of Congress Cataloging-in-Publication Data
Kompare, Derek, 1969–
 CSI / Derek Kompare.
   p. cm. – (Wiley-Blackwell series in film and television)
 Includes bibliographical references and index.
   ISBN 978-1-4051-8609-4 (hardcover : alk. paper) – ISBN 978-1-4051-8608-7 (pbk. : alk. paper) 1. CSI, crime scene investigation (Television program) 2. Television–Social aspects–United States.   I. Title.
 PN1992.77.C75K66 2010
 791.45′72–dc22
                                                         2010016195

A catalogue record for this book is available from the British Library.

Set in 10.5/13pt Minion by SPi Publisher Services, Pondicherry, India
Printed in Singapore by Ho Printing Singapore Pte Ltd

001 2010

Contents

List of Figures	vi
Acknowledgments	ix
Introduction: Why *CSI* Matters	1
1. Science, Spectacle, and Storytelling	8
2. What Happens in *CSI*'s Vegas	36
3. Finding Balance: Professionalism in Serial Narrative	55
4. *CSI* Effects	80
Conclusion	102
Appendix: *CSI* Episode Guide, 2000–9	105
Notes	129
References	135
Index	137

List of Figures

Crime and investigation: Catherine and Grissom investigate
a dead body in a Strip hotel room — 11

Teamwork: Sara and Nick discuss a case as they walk
through the crime labs — 13

Arriving at the scene: Catherine and Grissom search for
clues late at night on a desert highway — 27

Investigation: Sara and Warrick piece together the chain of
events in a road accident — 29

Investigation: Warrick attempts to match a blown-up
film image of the Stratosphere Tower to the view from a
dilapidated hotel room, in order to find the scene of the crime — 29

Transparent science and justice: Sara and Hodges discuss
evidence in the lab — 31

The autopsy room: Grissom and Doc Robbins diagnose
the cause of death (COD) — 32

The interrogation room: Catherine and Brass confront the
suspicious parents of a dead child — 33

The Strip, in nocturnal glory — 40

Death in Sin City: Grissom and Brass at another
apparent murder in a Strip hotel — 43

Sam Braun, icon of Old Vegas, keeping secrets from Catherine	50
Death in the Wilderness: Grissom, Catherine, and Brass at a triple murder scene in the Mojave Desert	52
Death in the Wilderness: Grissom studies a headless body buried up to its shoulders in a remote forest	53
Soulmates, or kindred intellects?: Grissom and Lady Heather get intimate	61
Through one-way glass, Sara sees Grissom obliquely confess his feelings for her	62
Searching for "the rush": Catherine searching for an incriminating frame of film	65
Fleeting connection: Catherine and Warrick share an (almost) intimate moment, helping fuel fan speculation about their unrequited passions	68
Tenacity: Sara investigates every scrap of evidence at the scene of the accident	70
Focus: Warrick tests a ladder for blood traces	72
Empathy: Nick calmly gets a teen boy to confess to masturbation, in order to account for traces of semen found on a shirt in the suspect's house	75
Exuberance: Greg triumphantly shows off an incriminating evidence sample	77
Reality/fiction: Technical consultant and former criminalist Elizabeth Devine displays real lab equipment on the CSI set, like this polarized light microscope	94
Watching the detectives: Catherine and Grissom encounter a reality TV camera crew	96
Mediated justice: Brass, Grissom and Warrick meet the press after the arrest of Hollywood star Tom Havilland	97

Public justice: Greg faces the media after the mixed findings
of the coroner's inquest which ruled the death of
Demetrius James "excusable" 100

Forensic science on trial: Warrick is cross-examined
about a knife found in a defendant's car 101

Acknowledgments

Researching and writing about an individual, though long-running, television show has been a particular challenge, and I am very grateful to those who have assisted me along the way.

First, I cannot thank enough the series editors, Diane Negra and Yvonne Tasker, for their support and guidance throughout this process. Their understanding, encouragement, and comments helped provide a supportive environment throughout its development, and ultimately made this a stronger book. Similarly, I must thank Wiley-Blackwell's acquisition editor Jayne Fargnoli for introducing me to this book series, and for her support of all of its titles.

I am grateful to the Division of Cinema-Television and the Meadows School of the Arts at Southern Methodist University for allowing me a research leave that enabled me to thoroughly research *CSI* and begin writing this book. The time spent researching crime fiction and the history of Las Vegas, and viewing and annotating each episode was immeasurably valuable, and I am thankful for this academic support. This research work has also led me to create a new course on crime television, so my SMU students are already getting a return on their investment!

I must also acknowledge the unconditional support of my family: my children Ben and Rose, and especially my wife Sally, for putting up with my obsessive viewing routines and persistent work schedule for many months. Similarly, I thank my brother John for hosting me in Las Vegas for several days, and showing me around many facets of this fascinating city. Creative projects are shared not only by those who create, but also by those who live with the creators, and I am thankful that they have allowed me to share it with them.

Despite what one may think, an extensive analysis of a long-running TV series is not necessarily a pleasurable experience. Thus, I would also like to tip my hat to the cast and crew of *CSI*, for inciting my interest in this intriguing series nine years ago, and consistently delivering on its promise in surprising and rewarding ways for over 200 episodes. It has indeed been a pleasure, and I hope this study can contribute to an appreciation and understanding of this engrossing, classic and popular (yet still relatively overlooked) series.

Introduction
Why CSI Matters

Bodies tell a story because we interpret them the way our predecessors taught us to. Just because we don't see something we're supposed to see doesn't mean that it's not there.
(Grissom, 2.3, "Overload")[1]

On the surface, *CSI: Crime Scene Investigation* (CBS, 2000–) appears nearly identical to the dozens of crime-based television dramas that preceded it. A murder has apparently occurred. The police investigate. The crime is solved. The guilty are brought to justice. The pattern is well entrenched in popular culture, and particularly on TV. However, as chief crime scene investigator Gil Grissom tells his team of criminalists (science-trained forensic investigators, also known as CSIs) we must look more closely at the available evidence. What seemed obvious at first is now thick with meaning and mystery. A murder has apparently occurred ... but why is the blood spatter on the walls from someone else? The police investigate ... spending as much time in the lab as on the street. The crime is solved ... only after the painstaking processing of a wide array of evidence, from crushed cars to human DNA. The guilty are caught ... but they have yet to be tried in court. *CSI* takes the formula of classic detective fiction, extending from literature to television, and injects it with conspicuous spectacle and style, creating a contemporary mythos of science and the law, and enthralling tens of millions of regular viewers.

However, despite its great cultural and industrial success over the past decade, *CSI* has never been much of a critical darling. While it has rarely met with outright derision, it is widely regarded as workmanlike, and considered the epitome of unchallenging, "by-the-numbers" television in some quarters. As Steven Cohan points out in his monograph on the series, CSI "has not achieved high visibility as either a critical favorite or cult show" (2008: 4).[2] Indeed, the term "another CSI" has become a euphemism for broadcast network conservatism, in much the same way "another Mad Men" has indicated the opposite quality, that is, cable network innovation. Such dismissive treatment sells the series far short, denying its formal and ideological achievements, as well as its pleasures. While the series is indeed "formulaic" (to take one common epithet), that formula is itself a rich, deep text, built upon a long history of spectacle, crime fiction, and melodrama, and a more contemporary tableau of high technology, excessive style, and professional ethics. The dismissal of CSI ignores how even mainstream, crowd-pleasing television is a complex dance of many factors, and fails to understand its impact on television and popular culture more broadly in the 2000s. I am not arguing that CSI is important only because it is watched by tens of millions of people every Thursday night; rather, I believe it is important because it is one of the decade's most formally intriguing and influential cultural texts. It has not topped many critics' lists, won Emmys (though it has been nominated), nor (until recently, at least) attracted much scholarly attention, but it has undoubtedly changed the standards and expectations of procedural drama and televisual style, and has contributed to public debates about science, technology, professionalism, and criminal justice.

As it happens, it is also one of television's most consistently engaging series. While *The Sopranos* (HBO, 1999–2007), *Lost* (ABC, 2004–10), *The Wire* (HBO, 2002–8), *Battlestar Galactica* (Sci-Fi, 2003–9), and *Mad Men* (AMC, 2007–) have had to function with stratospheric narrative and stylistic expectations with virtually every new episode, CSI has quietly (or as quietly as a top-five series can get) dominated its more modest terrain: episodic detective stories, with a touch of horror, comedy, melodrama, and serialized professional and personal angst. Ten years on, while it may have slipped up on occasion (e.g., Nick's season six haircut), it continues to deliver on its promise.

At points in long runs where other series are generally exhausted, *CSI* has mined new veins of drama and spectacle. The fact that its seventh season (2006–7) is arguably its best speaks volumes for its consistency in this regard. Moreover, it has done this with largely the same creative team it started out with a decade ago.

As a popular and formally dense text, *CSI* thus challenges our assumptions about the role and power of mass-appeal television in the "post-network" era of the 2000s, as narrowcast channels and programming have commanded most critical and industrial attention.[3] The dominant trend in both mainstream and academic television criticism during this time has been towards what may be regarded as "art TV": programs which have garnered critical attention – and small, loyal, and (not unimportantly) affluent audiences – precisely for their divergence from "typical" television conventions. As HBO's famous slogan put it, these are programs that are somehow "not TV." While there are certainly antecedents for both such programming and such critical attention (such as *Homicide: Life on the Street* (1993–9), *Twin Peaks* (1990–1) or even the MTM dramas of the 1980s), the current cycle arguably begins with HBO's *The Sopranos* in 1999, a morally and aesthetically complex drama about a New Jersey mobster and his colleagues and family. The critical success of the series inspired the development of similarly audacious serial dramas throughout the 2000s, including, among many others throughout broadcast and cable television, HBO's *Six Feet Under* (2001–5), FX's *The Shield* (2002–8), ABC's *Lost*, and Sci-Fi's *Battlestar Galactica*. Each of these series has been taken up by both journalistic and academic critics as examples of the medium's maturation, and even as evidence of a new television "golden age."[4]

The emphasis in much of this academic criticism has been on the television text, that is, on the formal qualities of programs (and particularly on their narrative styles). While this move has certainly enriched our understanding of television form, it has also separated criticism a bit from an approach that focuses on how television functions as *popular culture*, that is, as media that successfully connects with sizable populations by resonating with its interests and identities. However, as the development of television drama, in particular, thus far in the twenty-first century has indicated, "popular television" is an increasingly ambiguous concept. Audience fragmentation has greatly diminished popular television's ceiling – its largest audience. As recently as the mid-1990s, the top-rated series on American TV (like NBC's long-running *ER*) could command over 40 million viewers a week. By the end of the 2000s, the top-rated show on TV, Fox's *American Idol*, typically drew around 20 million viewers. Put another way, *American Idol*, the most-watched show on American television, is a series that over 90% of Americans never watch. Moreover, while ratings are certainly not a transparent indicator of a series' popular success, they are still the primary currency upon which the television industry revolves. The ceiling and floor of acceptable ratings may have both lowered over the past 20 years, but the name of the game is still getting more viewers (and particularly more 18–49 year old viewers) than the other channels. Increasingly, however, the ratings are only one industrial and cultural measure of how a series is faring. Programs may also be gauged by how they are recorded and played back on DVRs, viewed on on-demand channels or streaming network (or licensed) websites, downloaded (legitimately or not), and sold on DVD. In addition, as Jonathan Gray (2010) argues, the *paratexts* of a program – its surrounding promotional materials, ancillary products, fan discourses, and critical coverage – may also extend its ostensible "popularity" even wider and/or deeper.

By any of these industrial measures, *CSI* is clearly popular television. At the time of this writing, it has been a top 10 network series for each of its 10 seasons, a top five series for eight seasons, and was the top-rated series on TV for two consecutive seasons (2002–4), drawing over 26 million weekly viewers at its peak. It has inspired two high-rated and long-running spinoffs (*CSI: Miami* [CBS, 2002–], and *CSI: NY* [CBS, 2004–]), and has reshaped the CBS prime-time schedule in its image.[5] Its reruns continue to draw viewers on cable networks and broadcast stations, and its DVDs continue to be purchased by fans. It has prolonged and expanded the forensic investigation subgenre on reality TV, on programs like *Cold Case Files* (1999–) and *Forensic Files* (1996–). Off the screen, it has inspired licensed museum exhibits, novels, comic books, video games, and even old-school pinball machines. Simply put, *CSI* is, by industry standards, the most successful dramatic television franchise of the past decade.

While such industrial factors have been key to its longevity as an entertainment product, they do not exhaust the definition of its popularity. Popular television is not only popular merely because many people watch it; it is also popular – in the sense of "relating to the people" – because of how it works as mass-appeal television. This is where the formal analyses of the so-called "aesthetic turn" in television studies can help illuminate our understanding of the series. While much of this work has focused on the supposed exceptions to television's formal and narrative norms, surely it is also useful to understand the rules themselves, in any era's most iconic texts. Norms, after all, are not static, and are as much products of their times as are the texts and codes that break them. If narrative and stylistic ambiguity is the yardstick, *CSI* is not a "groundbreaking" series in the manner of *The Sopranos*, *The Wire*, or *Lost*. Nor is it renowned for the playful excesses that animate *Glee* (Fox, 2009–), *Pushing Daisies* (ABC, 2007–8), and *Buffy the Vampire Slayer* (WB/UPN, 1997–2004). However, it is still a formally rich and rewarding text in its own right, inhabiting a kind of extra-realism (which I describe in the next chapter as a "heightened verisimilitude") whereby the conventional codes of narrative realism apply, but are first worked through an expressive and eclectic palette of audiovisual styles. Scenes on *CSI*, as befitting the series' emphasis on investigation, are oversaturated with *visibility*: spaces are expressively lit and staged, details are crisp and to the point, and expository dialogue smoothly directs our attention and comprehension. These overcharged elements, whether expressive lighting, slow-motion cinematography, pedagogical conversations, or CGI-enhanced gunshot wounds, heighten the series' investigation plots by amplifying our own practices of looking. As Cohan states, "the style reinforces what the investigative narratives dramatize, namely, the unimpeachable value of scientific vision" (2008: 57). We are encouraged to relish its sumptuous aesthetic display, and share in its principal characters' insatiable pursuit of "evidence." In these ways, *CSI* is unapologetically comfort food television: heavy on spectacle and drama, but still easy to digest.

This book analyzes *CSI* as a key example of popular, mainstream American broadcast network television in the early twenty-first century. It approaches the series as a set of representations: of science, of the justice system, of place, of professionalism, and of its own mediation. *CSI* conveys these representations in direct, mainstream, and surprisingly frank and moving mini-dramas of crimes and investigations, as well as the larger maxi-drama of its protagonists' careers and lives. *CSI*'s achievements as a popular network drama refute the argument that interesting television is only produced on boutique channels, or only for limited audiences.

The first chapter focuses on *CSI*'s narrative and audiovisual style. While the series conspicuously draws from the familiar lineage of the detective story, as a drama concerning forensic scientists it also focuses squarely on the issue of visibility. On *CSI*, the evidence is out there, and only the criminalists are properly trained and equipped to find it, process it, and successfully use it to get suspects charged with crimes. The series offers its evidence in spectacular fashion, from mutilated bodies to surreal flashbacks to musically-enhanced investigations. Along the way, this spectacle is meticulously structured by a standard narrative formula that foregrounds practices of visibility (e.g., forensic investigation, confession, etc.), and leads to the final revelation of the guilty.

CSI is notable as well for its setting. While most crime series have historically been set in New York, Los Angeles, or various anonymous "big cities," *CSI* focuses on one of the most storied, controversial, and unique locales in America: Las Vegas, Nevada. Chapter 2 examines how the series has used Las Vegas in four distinct ways throughout its run, which collectively build a multi-faceted, yet familiar, representation of the city. *CSI*'s Vegas is certainly the "Sin City" of fame, dominated by casino gambling, luxury, and licensed "excessive" behavior. However it's also an everyday, growing city of 2 million people trying to get by much as anyone, anywhere, would do. Las Vegas also has a relatively short but colorful "old Vegas" past of gangsters, glitz, and gambling from the 1930s through 1970s, whose ghosts sometimes still haunt the city and our main characters. Finally, Las Vegas is emblematic of the American southwest, where deserts, mountains, and small towns present intriguing challenges that would not be found in most other settings. Crime affects each of these aspects of Las Vegas, and the *CSI* team works in all of them.

While *CSI* is considered more of an "episodic" series, in that its primary focus is on the cases at hand in any individual episode, it also has an important, if subtle, serialized component. Chapter 3 examines the lives of its six primary characters: Gil Grissom, Catherine Willows, Sara Sidle, Nick Stokes, Warrick Brown, and Greg Sanders. Each of these characters changes over the course of the series, and their relationships with each other and their work dramatize the impact of professional obligations on everyday lives. Accordingly, though its moments of character focus are relatively rare in comparison to the boutique dramas mentioned above, *CSI* is ultimately as much about contemporary adulthood as it is about solving murders. On *CSI*, heart and head must be balanced, or else one runs the oft-stated risk of burnout, or of "getting too involved."

Finally, *CSI* is also an influence beyond the TV screen, and has allegedly fostered several trends throughout popular and political culture. Primary among these is the "*CSI* effect," which has arguably caused jurors to hold unreasonably high expectations of forensic investigations, based on their viewing of such procedures on *CSI* and similar series. In the final chapter, I argue that in order to better understand this ostensible "*CSI* effect," it is important to take into account how such claims form and develop. Thus, there are several "*CSI* effects" that have resulted from the series' smash success, including the development of a multimedia entertainment franchise, and the impact of its representations on the real criminal justice system. It is important as well to understand how the series itself posits its own relationships with the public, the media, and other parts of the government, both within its texts, and in its behind-the-scenes materials. *CSI* is as much about the representation of crime and investigation as it is about the work itself.

A short note on titles used here; in the interests of flow, I have shortened episode titles down to their number, indicated by season and episode number. Thus, 4.8 refers to season four, episode eight ("After The Show"). A full list of episodes in seasons one through nine, including airdates and key credits, is included in the appendix.

Chapter 1

Science, Spectacle, and Storytelling

> *My only real purpose is to be smarter than the bad guys, to find the evidence that they did not know they left behind, and make sense of it all.* (Grissom, 3.6, "The Execution of Catherine Willows")[1]

Near the end of a typical *CSI* episode, after being confronted with the details of their crime as reassembled by Grissom's team, over-confident suspects will react with a mixture of admiration and incredulity. They are impressed with the criminalists' ability to piece together the narrative of their crime, but fearful of its effect upon their legal guilt or innocence. "That's a good story," they tell the accusing investigator. This final, theatrical act of denial is a common trope of crime fiction, and *CSI* embraces it, as it does with so many other such generic trappings. Its crimes and investigations are, in fact, "good stories," and even our skepticism as jaded TV viewers is insufficient to derail our enjoyment at the story told.

How does *CSI* do it? How does it work as a platform for mass audience storytelling, especially in an era when that very concept is increasingly dubious? It is certainly fair to say that *CSI* works because it is virtually note-perfect popular television drama, in the historical tradition, regularly delivering an accessible yet intriguing mix of mystery, education, and esprit de corps. It's undeniably the product of a particularly baroque production style, largely courtesy of Jerry Bruckheimer, the producer who sought to bring his assertive big-screen bravado to television; Danny Cannon, the director who precisely set this tone in the first season; and a meticulous production crew, who have materialized these values for over 200 episodes. It also comes from a well-honed television storytelling craft, from Anthony Zuiker, who conceived the series, and Carol Mendelsohn, Ann Donahue, Naren Shankar, and all the other writers (including former crime scene investigators Richard Catalani and Elizabeth Devine), who skillfully narrativize crime, science, spectacle, and professionalism in each episode. It's also the result of consistently effective performances from regular cast members William Petersen, Marg Helgenberger, Jorja Fox, George Eads, Gary Dourdan, Eric Szmanda, Paul Guilfoyle, and many recurring and guest actors. All told, the series has deservedly established itself as one of the key formal and industrial paradigms in mainstream American television, circa 2000–10. However, *CSI*'s roots actually lie deeper, in the long, entwined histories of science, bureaucratic power, official justice, crime fiction, and media spectacle. The series is both classic and contemporary, coupling long-standing crime narrative tropes with state-of-the-art twenty-first century tools, techniques and visual storytelling. This chapter "follows the evidence" of *CSI*'s style, tracing how crime and investigation plots are conveyed through conspicuous spectacle, and how this formal commitment structures the series' standard narrative formula.

Crime and Investigation

At the risk of opening with a banal observation, I'll point out that the C in *CSI* stands for "crime." While we most often take this term for granted, it is worth considering what "crime" means. Crimes are essentially cultural: actions or states of being deemed "deviant" and/ or "dangerous," and thus "criminalized," that is, placed outside the boundaries of "normal" society, however that may be defined in particular contexts (and by particular forces, of which the sovereign State is only one). Crimes are therefore highly contingent. Actions deemed "criminal" (e.g., gambling) in one place may fall within the realm of normality in others (e.g., Las Vegas). As Michel Foucault points out in *Discipline and Punish*, the criminal justice system, as we typically regard it in the twenty-first century, is largely a product of scientific, medical, and bureaucratic state powers that began to coalesce over 200 years ago. Thus, "criminal" activities and people are the purview of the government and its agents (including scientists of various stripes). That said, as the phrase "a crime of passion" neatly evokes, we also take for granted that crime also occurs on the scale of individual lives. To take an archetypal example, one person's death at the hands of another is not only a public matter for the court: it is regarded as a violation of private trust.

Accordingly, with such public and private consequences indicated by its very definition, crime has long fueled the interest of outside observers. While there are many historical and mythical antecedents, this interest becomes particularly active alongside modernity, beginning in the eighteenth century, when accounts of prison confessions, detailing crimes in graphic detail, were first published in books and periodicals. These precursors, to what we today refer to as "true crime" narratives, indicate a strong relationship between crime, spectacle (even in the written word alone), narrative, and official and popular consumption. In other words, crime began to function as both a category of State power and mass entertainment. By the mid nineteenth century, fictional crime stories clearly inspired by these accounts began to be published, detailing not only crimes but also their investigations by interested or official authorities. As John Scaggs describes in his history of crime fiction, the "rational detective," first seen in the Dupin stories of Edgar Allan Poe in the 1840s, is a particularly modern character, schooled in the actions, objects and methods of post-Enlightenment civilization, and most often ensconced in its legal and moral codes, as well as its bureaucracy (2005: 33–49). Appearing in society virtually simultaneously with organized police departments, and replacing the clerical or royal decree of crime with intensive observation and logical deduction, detectives, even amateur or independent ones, were represented as agents of modernity in literature, solving crimes and reasserting the prevailing moral and social order, however contentious that may be.

Moreover, they did so increasingly through the new theories and tools of forensic science, including photography, fingerprinting, and even lie detectors: all modern technologies and methods ostensibly

Crime and investigation: Catherine and Grissom investigate a dead body in a Strip hotel room, in 4.1 "Assume Nothing."

designed to identify criminal individuals. As Ronald R. Thomas notes in his study of the concomitant rise of detective fiction and forensic criminology, the "detective narrative, in its deployment of these forensic technologies and in its resemblance to them, helped to make nineteenth-century persons legible for a modern technological culture" (1999: 17). This burgeoning "modern technological culture" of the late nineteenth and early twentieth centuries was defined by the new technologies and scientific methods of visibility. Technologies like photography, cinematography, and sound recording created new registers of spectacle, freezing in time and space moments – like Eadweard Muybridge's famous 1878 photos of Leland Stanford's galloping horse – that were once only fleeting, and disseminating mass-produced copies to far-flung viewers and listeners. Similarly, rapidly developing fields like biology, medicine, chemistry, and physics had begun to re-envision the world as a rational system of signs that could be made visible through increasingly precise scientific methods of experimentation and observation. By the beginning of the twentieth century, these practices, theories, and devices had redefined the world, down to the atom, as the realm of the visible.

Within a few decades, after a century of increasingly modern urban, bureaucratic, and scientifically-ordered life in the most developed countries, crime fiction, in many sub-genres, had become one of the primary forms of popular storytelling in literature, comics, film, drama, and radio. Detectives, empowered with modern tools and methods, and operating in the new scientific and legal regimes of the visible, imbued a more traditional moral certainty to an otherwise turbulent age. Unsurprisingly, the genre was readily adapted to television as early as the 1940s, its investigative narratives making an easy transition to the intimate, yet functionally civic properties of the new, domestic visual medium. There, as Jason Mittell has argued, the early critical and popular successes of *Dragnet* (1951–9), which stylistically drew from 1940s crime films and radio dramas, helped establish the generic template for TV crime drama, and in particular the police procedural (2004: 121–52). The genre has since become one of American television's staples. As such, it has continued the technocratic pursuit of the visible "truth" of crime, and has functioned as a prime exemplar of television's ideological construction of American society as a schizoid terrain of comfort and danger, where staid normality prevails, but "bad guys" also prey on "the innocent," with only the "thin blue line" of the police (or, their occasional substitutes, such as the conscientious private eye or vigilant national security agent/spy) positioned in between.

However, unlike the eccentric sleuths of classic crime fiction like Dupin, Sherlock Holmes, Miss Marple, or even television's own Columbo, who all practically work solo, displaying singular powers of perception, the investigators of *CSI*, like many (though not all) of their TV detective forebears, function as a team, grounding their actions firmly in the realm of State power and bureaucratic routine, complete with badges and insignia.[2] Similarly, while the classic rational detectives solved small murders on their own, seemingly removed from the bulk of society (e.g., in archetypal country houses), the *CSI* team – supervising CSI Gil Grissom (William Petersen), senior CSI Catherine Willows (Marg Helgenberger), and junior CSIs Warrick Brown (Gary Dourdan), Greg Sanders (Eric Szmanda), Sara Sidle (Jorja Fox), and

Teamwork: Sara and Nick discuss a case as they walk through the crime labs, in 4.7 "Invisible Evidence."

Nick Stokes (George Eads) – engages directly with every level of the social order in southern Nevada, seeking to restore public justice and normality where it has been disrupted. Each investigation they are involved with is an official case under the authority of the Las Vegas Metropolitan Police Department. Thus, the law, rather than the investigators' individual guile, ultimately determines their actions. Importantly, team members, including lab technicians and detectives, are also typically depicted as model public servants: selfless, reliable team players, with near-unimpeachable crime-solving skills (though also slightly flawed in certain ways that occasionally impede their abilities, as chapter 3 will examine). While individual egos may sometimes arise, investigations on *CSI* are always conceived of as a collective social action, serving a viable and *official* need: scientific expertise producing visible, criminal truth for the modern bureaucratic state.

As with most forms of crime fiction (with the notable exception of what Scaggs describes as the "crime thriller," which is generally centered on the actions and psychology of the criminal, rather than the detective), and in keeping with its roots in nineteenth-century science, technology, and bureaucracy, television crime drama is still primarily premised on the practice of investigation: that is, the generation and analysis of "evidence" which eventually links particular crimes to particular criminals. Protagonists in crime fiction must successfully gather and correctly study the available physical and psychological traces in order to apprehend the criminals. This is generally conveyed in a straightforward narrative formula, where the discovery of a crime leads immediately into its investigation, which only ends at the moment of revelation, when the criminals have been publicly revealed, and are arrested by the police or (less commonly) killed. The utility of this formula for series television, or for any media series, for that matter, is that it takes viewers (or readers, etc.) on a familiar, comfortable, ritualized narrative path. Each episode ostensibly functions like every other episode, with the same expectations and, ultimately, reassurances by the end. In these narrative worlds, while it's clear that crime will always happen, the "proper authorities," that is, those granted the requisite skills and/or official license, will (almost) always deal with it, and justice will (almost) always prevail. *CSI* unapologetically follows this classic formula, almost to the letter: crimes are discovered, evidence is investigated, and criminals are ultimately revealed.

It is important to note that "evidence" is both a scientific and legal category. In the laboratory, hypotheses are tested by observing experiments, that is, by producing measurable evidence. In the courtroom, guilt or innocence is proven, "beyond a reasonable doubt," through the logical weighing of each side's evidence. Ellen Burton Harrington points out that, in its veneration of evidence above all, *CSI*, as did Thomas' earlier detective stories, reaffirms the standard ideology of evidence in the service of both science and law, and particularly its deployment in the nineteenth century to fix the identity of criminals (2007). While the specific tools and methods of criminal investigation have changed since then, this initial rationale remains. As Martha Gever states in her study of the use of digital surveillance on *CSI*, as in the classic ideology of detection, individuals are "perceptible only as the sum of inscriptions," that is, the "evidence" ascribed to them (2005: 447). This unrelenting focus on the evidence as the engine of forensic science and criminal inscription drives *CSI*, down to its signature use of the Who's "Who Are You?" as its theme song.

The emphasis on evidence draws *CSI* even more intently to the concept of *spectacle*. A spectacle, broadly speaking, is something to behold with all of one's senses (not only visual), entrancing audiences with exciting sights, sounds, and other sensations. Critics have long considered visual and (more recently) audio spectacle to be a seminal component of the culture and industry of film, which emerged out of science and entertainment (e.g., the theater and the circus) at the turn of the twentieth century. As John Caldwell has argued, such conspicuous spectacle has also been a critical component in the functioning of television, as dominant industrial policy since the 1980s, and in its functioning since its inception (1995: 3–102). However, as the Marxist critic Guy Debord famously claimed, spectacle is also a key part of the fabric of contemporary society, "a social relation between people that is mediated by images" (1983: 7). As with the technocratic, intensely visible world produced by nineteenth- and twentieth-century science and bureaucracy, the very idea of spectacle structures our perceptions, presenting a normative expectation of arresting, or at least engaging, images and sounds. *CSI* narrates spectacle: from its darkness-piercing flashlights to its climactic confessions, its format is premised on processes of visibility, and its plots hinge on revelation. Accordingly, narrative and formal techniques of spectacle are both fully woven into the tasks of its characters (i.e., gathering and processing evidence), and conspicuously used in its production as fictional television (e.g., through the use of CGI, prosthetics, impressionistic editing, etc.).

Showing and Telling

Visibility is the primary component of television crime drama. While the crime itself might not have been seen in the narrative by anyone except the criminal and victims, its investigation is, by contrast, highly visible, and is focused on producing visibility, that is, revealing the intimate details of the crime. As both a narrative world and a television drama, *CSI*, as suggested by its full title – *Crime Scene Investigation* – is saturated with such visibility, which, as with spectacle in general, includes not only visual information, but may also involve the four other senses. On *CSI*, as with any film or television program, only sight and sound are actually present, but they can be effectively manipulated to suggest other senses, as when characters react to the putrid smell of a rotting corpse, for example (as seen in 3.18, 4.2, 5.3, 6.1, and others). Whether through performance, cinematography, editing, sound, or visual effects, *CSI* produces a wide range of visible events, objects, and people. Visibility leads the police and criminalists to crime scenes, propels their investigations, and ultimately confirms or denies their suspicions. Most importantly, it also shapes our perceptions of narrative events, and propels narrative enigmas: what lies behind the secret door? Whose decapitated head is in the helmet? What caused that bruising? In *CSI*, visibility comes in many forms and through many sources, both complementary, as with ballistics testing that confirms that a particular gun was fired, and contradictory, when witnesses recall different versions of an event. It ranges in scope from demolished buildings to DNA. Moreover, it is quite often initially *in*visible, as with blood traces on a bathroom sink, or a few hairs on a car seat.

At the level of narrative action, however, and as a prominent manifestation of popular broadcast television in the early twenty-first century, *CSI* is more concerned with the implications of the concept of visibility, and of particular acts and practices of visibility, than with what is ultimately "revealed." In other words, it is the technologies of visibility, and the skills of the investigators (as well as the series' production personnel), rather than the resolution of crimes that legitimates viewer interest. Thus, the process, rather than the outcome, of investigation, is *CSI*'s *raison d'être*. Martha Gever argues that "the locus of truth in *CSI* resides in expert applications of scientific technologies that organize and produce inscriptions, without troubling with problems of interpretation" (2005: 456). The same might be said of the production of *CSI* as a television show: impressive spectacle is meticulously and skillfully assembled, and left at that. Technologies of inscription, whether DNA analysis databases, mass spectrometers, film cameras, or post-production suites, produce the spectacular "truths" that drive *CSI*.

As the criminalists – Grissom in particular – state throughout the series, evidence – both the physical material gathered, described, and displayed in multiple and intricate ways throughout every episode, and the narrative material of witnesses – is key. Accordingly, visibility in *CSI*, centered on the idea of evidence, is structured around *showing* and *telling*: traces of criminal activity both conspicuously displayed *and* conspicuously described. While we rarely witness – in narrative chronology, at least – the actual incidents that propel each episode's investigations, we perceive them repeatedly through reassembled traces with each new piece of evidence. Similarly, while we see a great deal of evidence gathering and processing (in extensive and elaborate montage sequences; see below), we are often only told the results of these tasks, as, for example, lab tech David Hodges hands CSI Nick Stokes a piece of paper with the results of paint chip tests and tells him the make, model, and year of the car they are seeking. At other moments, however, we are both shown and told a great deal about the phenomena or event under examination. This is most commonly seen in Doc Robbins' autopsy scenes, as he explains and indicates the victims' causes of death in graphic detail. Bodies are displayed (inside and out), probed, dissected, and described in this manner in nearly every episode. As Robbins describes the cause of death, the camera zooms into the body, and Robbins' explanation is re-enacted with prosthetics and/or CGI effects: tissue is punctured, bones are crunched, lungs are drowned, spines are severed, and so on. We, alongside the investigating criminalist (usually Grissom in these scenes), are thus elegantly made to understand exactly what happened to kill the victim – that is, the cause of death, or "COD" in CSI-speak – in a couple of minutes of screen time, with little hesitation or uncertainty.

As these autopsies also indicate, showing and telling on *CSI* is not only about exposition or plot resolution, however, as every episode also features several moments and even entire scenes that function more precisely as *pedagogy*, that is, as classic visual-verbal teaching. Information is not merely presented: it is rendered spectacular, and reinforced by the narrative. Whether describing bruising patterns, tool marks, bullet velocities, toxicity of poisons, blood spatter range, conduction of electricity, properties of digital video, blackjack betting, the physical strength of a horse's front legs, or any other obvious or arcane subject, *CSI* constantly *teaches* us about its world. The question of whether or not the content of such instruction is actually valid outside the series is significant (as chapter 4 will examine), but ultimately beside the point. In its dazzling immediate application, it works: we are effectively "educated" by these moments, at least as far as the narrative requires us to be. John Hartley argues that television, as a domestic, public, centralized audiovisual medium, can be extremely effective in such pedagogical moments, enough so that "teaching" should be considered the medium's primary function. "[Television]'s not *just* a teacher, it's a good one" (1999: 32).

The series' emphasis on the production of visibility, coupled with this earnest pedagogy, and an excessively aestheticized *mise-en-scène* function together to produce a *heightened verisimilitude*, whereby conspicuous spectacle enhances audiovisual appeal (i.e., the series' renowned "ear" and "eye candy"), propels the narrative, and even stakes some claims for technical accuracy. Although such a mix of stylized excess and functional realism may seem dubious or even irresponsible to some viewers wedded to traditional conceptions of television realism, it's perfectly consonant with the dominant stylistic sensibility of American television drama in the 2000s.[3] Accordingly, *CSI* easily and engagingly functions in an almost theatrical style, pushing just past the normative edges of television realism. Colors are slightly oversaturated, spaces are generally expressionistically lit, cameras seemingly float and glide, editing is conspicuous, and even performances are just a bit broader than prime-time dramatic norms. By extending the presentation of concepts, objects, or practices beyond the norms of conventional television realism, even as depicted in crime drama, *CSI* ratchets up viewers' potential aesthetic, emotional and rational investments. While some critics may value a more austere (though ultimately no less stylized; "austerity" itself being a style) approach to crime narrative, *CSI*'s "excessive" style, far from being a narrative hindrance, is appropriate to twenty-first century media culture, and particularly to dramatic television. In a fast-paced, screen-centered media age when cutting-edge CGI regularly illustrates news and documentary programming, and nearly 2 billion people routinely use the multiple-layered systems of representation on mobile phones, web browsers, and other platforms, mediated information normatively circulates in many ways. Thus, despite stylistic choices that seem "unrealistic" (e.g., slow motion, conspicuous post-processing, tangential effects sequences, perpetually shadowy lighting, dubious investigative technology, etc.), *CSI* can still effectively claim to be grounded in "real" twenty-first-century media culture. In his extended analysis of 4.8, Cohan argues that the series' meticulous visual style reflects its narrative ideology of visibility, exploring "the tension inherent in *CSI*'s fascination with looking at and through science" (2008: 86). As chapter 4 will show, this dominant sensibility, bolstered by promotional materials like cast and crew interviews and DVD behind-the-scenes features, has even allegedly fostered real effects on the expectations of actual forensic science technologies and practices.

CSI's signature gratuitous treatments of evidence are thus essential in its pursuit of heightened verisimilitude. The conventionally-visible world of people, objects and places in television crime drama – the usual eyewitness statements, gunshot wounds, fingerprints and confessions – is made even more visible on the series, stylized well past the boundaries of traditional generic realism. In addition, otherwise invisible realms – most notably, the interior of the human body – are routinely made visible in the series' signature "CSI shots," as the camera seemingly swoops down through impossibly small holes or even penetrates walls in order to see what lies beneath the surface. This visibility extends to the microscopic worlds of molecules, striations, alleles and the like, which are brought into sight with the cutting-edge imaging and analysis technology of forensic pathology, chemical trace analysis, ballistics, and, most significantly, DNA analysis. Data gleaned from this laboratory analysis is then typically searched in the narrative against nationally- and globally-networked databases such as AFIS (the Automated Fingerprint Identification System), CODIS (the Combined DNA Index System), and IBIS (the Interagency Border Inspection System), which are all presented not so much as resources but as gleaming, state-of-the-art Truth Machines, as all-knowable as the fictional future computers of the *Star Trek* universe.[4]

This gratuitous spectacle extends as well to the evidence of witness and suspect statements and investigators' speculations, which are not only told (verbally) but also shown in brief audiovisual sequences. Typically, these scenes go even further stylistically, discarding all the usual codes of realism in favor of more visceral and ambiguous regimes of light, color, motion, texture, and sound. For example, in 3.7, the "bullet time" effect ("freezing" action into three-dimensional space, also seen prominently in the flashforward of the lab shootout that opens 10.1) is used to speculate about a particular punch in a high-stakes boxing match. In 6.4, the prime suspect's version of her experiences in the UFO cult, and with its leader, is rendered in a distorted, nightmarish montage sequence. By equating evidence with spectacle in this manner, *CSI* treads a clear visual narrative path, with all made exciting, and nothing significant left unexplored or unexplained. As Karen Lury notes, this rendering of data into spectacle and back into data is one of the series' hallmark practices. "The tension between the power of the image and the power over the image is . . . the continual tease of this programme." (2005: 50). I would add to this that this "tension" persists at the meta-level as well, in the self-conscious production and promotion of *CSI*. In other words, this "image-power" is as much about *CSI* as popular television as it is the fictional CSIs on the series.

However intoxicating its spectacles, since *CSI* is ostensibly concerned with science, its pedagogical remit would not function without its protagonists' expository dialogue that teaches viewers what it all means. What is the significance of a particular insect on a decomposing body? What is the effect of this chemical on lung tissue? How do organized gamblers illegally affect the betting line on an upcoming basketball game? Most of us are not experts on most of what arises in the series' investigations; whether or not it is entirely accurate is irrelevant, as we have to accept it, and the CSIs' credibility, for the sake of the narrative. Telling, in this direct manner, is another factor that separates *CSI* from standard crime dramas. Again, it's the ideology of visibility, of the very production of "truth," that's more critical than whatever "truth" is ultimately presented. *CSI* justifies all this conspicuous explanation by making its protagonists teachers and students engaging in on-the-job training; we learn alongside them. The lower-ranked criminalists (Warrick Brown, Greg Sanders, Sara Sidle, and

Nick Stokes, for most of the series' run; Ronnie Lake, Riley Adams and Raymond Langston more recently) must consistently display their expertise and prowess to their supervisors (Gil Grissom and Catherine Willows) in order to maintain, and potentially advance, their careers. Grissom chides Sara and Nick for not knowing what "murder central" (the room nearest the stairs in a hotel) is in 2.11. In 5.1, the fact that Grissom calls out Greg's sloppiness in the investigation of the nightclub shooting serves as an important pedagogical moment for Greg, and for us; Grissom's authority is reaffirmed, as are our expectations of the team's (and thus the series') credibility. In the second half of season nine, Ray Langston must quickly come up to speed as a rookie CSI, and endures many such teaching moments in the field.

Importantly, however, these teacher-student roles are also not fixed. While Grissom is clearly the most professorial figure of the series, all the main characters display their expertise as the situation demands, as with Greg's often salacious (and quite possibly apocryphal) experiences in the Vegas club scene, Nick's fascination with vehicles and extreme sports, Warrick's deep knowledge of gambling, or Catherine's background as an exotic dancer. The series typically reinforces these explanations, which might otherwise seem highly tangential, through additional stylized audio-visual exposition, as in Doc Robbins' explanation of chakras in 2.17, Grissom's explanation of a roulette scam in 4.22, or Nick's elaborate courtroom reconstruction of Greg's actions at the scene of a near-fatal beating in the latter's coroner's inquest in 7.7.

Given that much of *CSI*'s investigations take the criminalists – and us – into worlds outside television's normative representations, these show-and-tell moments, justified primarily by the team's insatiable curiosity and stoic acceptance of almost all they encounter, and fueled by the series' signature conspicuous spectacle, aid our understanding while avoiding much of the moralizing generally typical of the crime genre. Both criminalists and viewers are encouraged to suspend their judgments of many depicted actions and practices, and instead, in classic scientific fashion, open their minds to broader possibilities. While much of these more subcultural scenes and storylines work in tandem with the depiction of Las Vegas as a kind of "anything goes" Sin City (as examined in chapter 2), they also function to bolster the team's standing as both scientists *and* cosmopolitans (at least within the borders of 2000s popular broadcast television). In other words, while some team members may react with surprise or even mild disgust at particular practices they encounter, they almost always move quickly on to acceptance, reinforcing their objectivity and their sophisticated sensibilities. As Cohan argues, in these plots and scenes "a continuing interrogation of normalcy turns the ethical compass of *CSI*" (2008: 123). For example, myriad sexual fetishes and subcultures are depicted in the series, their basic codes and rules explained to viewers in as explicit terms as prime time network television generally allows. Several episodes focus on BDSM, with the recurring dominatrix character of Lady Heather serving as the team's guide to this world. While some of these subcultures are met with some ridicule and/or skepticism from the regulars, Grissom, as moral and intellectual center, is generally insistent that people and practices be understood on their own terms. In 4.5, during an investigation of a murder at a "furries and plushies" convention, Grissom, citing Freud, notes that "the only unnatural sexual behavior [is] to have none at all."[5] In addition to sexual subcultures, the series also regularly delves into other non-mainstream worlds, giving them similarly extensive pedagogical treatments (again, within the conceptual confines of prime-time network television), including magic (3.5), haute cuisine (3.11, 8.2), Buddhism (2.17), and norteño narcocorrido music (5.12), as well as the even more esoteric realms of vampires (4.13), UFO cults (6.4, 7.22), murder groupies (3.22), and robot fighting (3.18).

Following the Evidence

As effective popular television, *CSI* is deceptively simple yet compelling. Throughout the series, Grissom often reminds his team to "follow the evidence." This directive, while narratively significant to them both in the moment and cumulatively, is also taken to heart by viewers. Individual episodes teach us how to read the series' presentation of "evidence"; additional episodes reward this lesson by conforming to our expectations. In principle, this is not only effective television storytelling; it is also effective science. While our materials are slickly-produced television episodes, as opposed to spattered blood drops or mysterious fibers, we share the criminalists' research methods, following the available evidence to solve the narratives/crimes in each episode.

Most episodes of *CSI* follow a straightforward narrative formula common to popular fiction, and particularly to popular television: an initial stasis is broken by an event that compels the protagonists to restore the social order. This circular form, common across many television genres, allows characters and settings to continue over time more-or-less unchanged by any particular event. For this reason, it is generally referred to as *episodic narrative*; each cycle of stasis-rupture-stasis conveying a distinct segment in the characters' lives, and an individual, almost interchangeable, portion of the series as a whole. By contrast, *serial narratives* consist of ongoing events told over many episodes, keeping events and characters' lives in flux. Episodes of serialized programs must therefore be viewed in a particular sequence in order to work; most American prime-time dramas since the 1980s have functioned in this manner. *CSI* straddles these forms by foregrounding the particularities of the cases at hand in each episode, while simultaneously, and more subtly, advancing serial storylines that may unfold across several episodes or even over several years.

Since they are premised on representing the process of problem-investigation-solution, procedural dramas like *CSI* utilize an episodic narrative style much more often than more serialized programs. Thus, the plots of most *CSI* episodes unfold similarly, in a standard narrative structure that explicitly foregrounds the process of investigation as a routine and methodical set of tasks carried out by knowledgeable and conscientious professionals. The particular narrative balance of *CSI*, tilted heavily in favor of episodic instead of serial storytelling, functions most pragmatically to provide an accessible format for a wide array of viewers. In every episode, casual viewers can get a complete crime-solving narrative delivered in less than an hour, while more loyal viewers can enjoy part of a much longer, subtler narrative exploring the challenges of working adulthood. This consistency, always coherently and engagingly conveyed, may arguably explain why *CSI* has been a top-rated series for virtually its entire run. It has never fallen out of the top 10, and has almost always finished in the top five most-watched regular series, regularly beaten out (in its first nine seasons) only by Fox's *American Idol* (2002–), ABC's *Dancing With The Stars* (2005–), and, occasionally, ABC's *Grey's Anatomy* (2005–).

While both episodic and serial form is essential to understanding how *CSI* works, the former is the primary concern here; chapter 3 will address the latter. The remainder of this chapter will analyze the three segments of *CSI*'s standard narrative – *Discovery, Investigation*, and *Revelation* – with an emphasis on how the extensive show-and-tell visibility described above shapes each.

Discovery

The purpose of most episodes' brief opening sequence is to locate us in the moment of discovery, when the stasis of "normal life" in Las Vegas is broken by the perception of crime. Usually, though not always, this sequence is set at nighttime, suggesting night as the normative setting of our narratives. Night is a critical component in the series' depiction of Las Vegas as "Sin City" (as discussed more fully in the next chapter), but is also justified in the narrative, as Grissom's team generally works the night shift at the crime lab.[6] More suggestively, night also conforms to the aesthetic and genre expectations of detective and suspense fiction, suggesting greater danger and mystery, and providing more opportunities for the production of visibility (e.g., in the ubiquitous form of flashlights illuminating the darkness). However, crime does not always work on the clock. Thus, to the series' credit, it also regularly explores the different possibilities of daytime crime scenes, when the veneer of everyday life is arguably more vulnerable, and the eruption of crime seemingly more distressing. The body buried in the park playground in 2.21, the car crashing into a crowded bistro in 3.17, and the deadly chase and shootout in 6.7 all show how violence, or the discovery of its traces in the form of dead bodies, can shatter the comfort of everyday life.

Regardless of the cases in the episode, the initial stasis at the opening of each episode is most often conveyed in a series of aerial shots of the Strip, Las Vegas' spectacular hub of hotels, casinos, and entertainment. A thunderous burst of sound marks the appearance of Vegas' gaudy buildings, as the camera floats over shots of the Strip, usually accompanied by the suggestive sounds of traffic, people, and the muted pinging of slot machines. On occasion, a song is used instead in these sequences to propel us into a particular sensibility, with shots of the Strip augmented or replaced by a thematic montage sequence (usually featuring one of that episode's victims). Particularly evocative examples of this approach include Prodigy's noisy "Spitfire" over scenes of Sin City in full effect in 5.1, Gary Jules' quiet lamentation "Mad World" with the slow-motion and split-screen comparison of a wealthy young playboy and a despondent laundry worker in 6.2, Frank Sinatra's version of "Almost Like Being In Love" over stock footage of "old Vegas" in 6.13, and, in 7.12, the Velvet Underground's classic "Sweet Jane," underscoring an elliptical montage of doomed young women arriving at the same Las Vegas bus station in 1975, 1989, 1999 and 2007. Such music-centered montage openings locate us not only geographically but emotionally, framing the visuals and setting us up for the remainder of the episode.

Recalling Alfred Hitchcock's famous opening shots of *Psycho* (1960), the visual perspective then typically moves in closer, in a combination of camera movement, editing, and visual effects, taking the viewer to a precise location where a crime is about to be perpetrated or discovered. Our consistent omniscient view of the narrative tableau (i.e., metropolitan Las Vegas) is reinforced this way in nearly every episode. We are given virtually universal visual access, as Vegas itself is fully revealed to us, moving through walls, buildings, and other obstacles as need be. The stylized production of visibility is thus presented from the very beginning of every episode. Most often the ultimate destination of this movement is a particular building or neighborhood, but it may also be in the desert or mountains surrounding the city. Eventually, we are close enough to observe people either caught up in deadly action, or, more commonly, stumbling upon the outcome of a seeming crime, such as a dead body or, not uncommonly, *part* of one (i.e., a severed and/or decomposed body part). Often the series plays with the expectations of both crime fiction and its own form by opening with potentially dangerous situations that are actually red herrings (i.e., narrative feints) that are suddenly derailed by the discovery of the real crime. For example, in 2.11, a seemingly imminent date rape in a late-night hotel lobby is cut off when the couple discovers an unconscious body in an elevator. In 6.17, a drunken woman stumbling from her car to her condo door is startled by a screaming and bloodied naked woman running down the hall. In 5.18, in a bit of double misdirection, a man on a wooded hillside at night at first appears to be a sniper setting up a hit, but is then revealed to be an amateur astronomer, who then gets caught in a sudden fireball rolling through the trees.

However, on rare occasions, the open may be *in media res* – that is, with the team already present on an investigation – or on a seemingly inexplicable scene, such as the courtroom open of 4.7, with Warrick on the stand; the *Seinfeld*-inspired diner breakfast in 6.21, as Greg, Nick and Sara philosophize about breakfasts and weddings; and the lab under attack in 10.1. On these occasions, the stasis is shifted back or forwards in story time, and we are forced to begin to piece together the events that brought the regular characters to that point. In the open of 4.12, for example, the suspense builds as a person slowly tracking through a darkened house is revealed to be Grissom already at a crime scene, whose initial reaction to the murder victim – a woman who bears an uncanny resemblance to Sara – is a critical plot point to the episode.

As soon as the discovery is made, the location is rendered a "crime scene" by the narrative and the action usually immediately cuts to a point after the police have arrived. They have already cordoned off the area – the "scene" is set, with the signature yellow tape marking its boundaries. The CSI team arrives, and their investigation begins.

Investigation

The term "crime scene" is especially apt for television drama, as the dramatic tableau of the case is defined, or at least initiated, by what is physically found (and thus, potentially visible) at that location.

Arriving at the scene: Catherine and Grissom search for clues late at night on a desert highway, in 4.5 "Fur and Loathing."

Investigations are the primary narrative action of the series, and typically take up 30 minutes of every 43-minute episode. However, since this is *CSI*, and not *Columbo*, or *Dragnet*, or even *Law & Order*, investigation is conspicuously rooted in scientific (or at least pseudo-scientific) principles, methods, and technologies. The series boldly states that physical evidence is all, and this focus justifies both the series' production of spectacle and its pedagogy: seeing really *is* believing. Appropriately, a great deal of the drama in the series is typically conveyed by medium and close-up shots of the team members *looking*. We watch their gazes, deciphering concentration in their furrowed brows and pursed lips. Importantly, we often do not immediately realize exactly what they are looking at or for. The sense conveyed by their focused actions (intense examinations of floors and walls, methodical usage of flashlights, painstaking searches through trash bags, squinting, etc.) is that they'll know what's important when they find it. When they do find something important, the camera, following their gaze, often cuts or zooms in to one of the series' signatures, a "*CSI* shot": an extreme close-up of a drop of blood, a single hair, a button, etc. Again, the critical narrative factor here is the production of visibility. All the objects the CSIs accumulate and record at the crime scene – bone fragments, shell casings, carpet fibers, diaries, and so on – become "evidence" by the very act of their gathering. Even the victims' time-of-death (aka "TOD"), routinely determined by assistant coroner David Phillips' thermometer at the scene, is immediately recorded and entered into evidence.

Importantly, beyond their eyes, ears, noses, hands, and occasionally tongues, the CSIs conspicuously use a wide variety of tools to extract evidence in the field, much of which would be otherwise invisible to immediate human perception. These tools are deployed in spectacular sequences that emphasize, and even eroticize, visibility even further, beyond normal human perception. Blood is magically made to appear on otherwise innocuous-looking surfaces and objects by a few sprays of phenolphthalein solution, which turns pink on contact. Semen – the second most-prevalent bodily fluid on the series – glows blue on examined sheets and clothing seen under ultraviolet (UV) light. Shoeprints are lifted intact onto static-charged plastic sheets. Fibers, scraps of cloth, paint flecks, and other miniscule bits of material are carefully bagged and collected. Photographs are taken from every angle, and surveillance tapes examined. Odors are even "recorded" as evidence, as with the incriminating perfume in 2.4. The series' pedagogical function, and full scope of show-and-tell, comes to the fore in the midst of all this observing, gathering and measuring. In these dazzling sequences, the scientific method is not only a means to plot ends; it is made to perform. In the past, and in other current crime series, these sorts of narrative actions would take place in ellipsis, almost entirely off-screen. The results of laboratory tests would be hastily passed on to police detectives, who would be our primary narrative agents. On *CSI*, by contrast, the very process of investigation is the key point of the show. Thus, actions that would be mundane, tedious and likely exhausting in real life (e.g., field searches, autopsies, lab experiments), or rendered off-screen, are instead showcased: conveyed in alluring, tightly choreographed and edited sequences. In 2.18, Sara and Warrick's grueling search down the highway for evidence linked to the bus crash becomes a deep-focus, dissolve-laden testament to their capabilities and diligence. In 7.20, Hodges' fascination with one of the serial killer's miniatures is represented by figuratively shrinking him down to its size, and following his search

SCIENCE, SPECTACLE, AND STORYTELLING   29

Investigation: Sara and Warrick piece together the chain of events in a road accident, in 2.18 "Chasing The Bus."

Investigation: Warrick attempts to match a blown-up film image of the Stratosphere Tower to the view from a dilapidated hotel room, in order to find the scene of the crime, in 3.8 "Snuff."

within that space. In 3.8, the team's methodical search for the hotel room where the snuff film was shot (based on a brief view of the Stratosphere Tower in a few frames of film) is conveyed through a long montage sequence taking them through many different rooms.

While these sequences rarely feature dialogue, music is a particularly important factor in them, and usually comes in the form of moody songs selected by music supervisor Jason Alexander. Citing his pursuit of music that has "a more organic and meandering feel to it," Alexander claims that he and the producers have "always tried to have a musical marriage between the cool exciting things they do in their job and what they're doing in their lab. Music is often with them on a journey of discovery, where they're finding things out" (White, 2008: 78). Typical songs in these sequences are rhythmic, mid-tempo tracks that generally fall in the broad category of "chill" music, from artists including Lamb, Radiohead, Sigur Ros, and Tosca. The resulting emotional tone is contemplative, yet active, reinforcing the sequences' shots of methodical, demanding investigation. Such work is thus made serious yet sexy: done by attractive people, in interesting settings, with cool music.[7]

Production design is a particularly important component of the investigation portion of episodes, reinforcing the series' heightened verisimilitude. While all the other spaces on the series are similarly "enhanced" visually in a standard way (deep depth of field, moody lighting, slightly saturated colors), the spaces of the Las Vegas Police Department – several labs, the autopsy room, a break room, Grissom's office, the interrogation room, and a few hallways – are the only standing sets on the series, and effectively serve as *CSI*'s primary dramatic tableaux. Visibility is foregrounded in the design of this space. Most of the walls shown in the station consist of large windows, some of them even floor-to-ceiling. This makes almost every room virtually transparent, or at least potentially transparent (blinds are sometimes partially or fully drawn), open to others' surveillance. The station is thus presented as an "open" space, with seemingly very few closed doors and secrets, where people freely enter and exit rooms, and discuss cases in the hall. Although contrary to our expectations of such centers of social authority, this design renders it an idealized space for positive perceptions of such a powerful social institution: literally "transparent," its inhabitants visually laboring on processing the evidence and thus serving justice. Information is even typically shared in these spaces, and people interact in a fairly open manner.

Transparent science and justice: Sara and Hodges discuss evidence in the lab, in 4.4 "Feeling The Heat."

However, within this general design, there are a few exceptions: rooms of limited access, limited visibility, as well as the inevitable barriers and hoops of modern bureaucracies. The autopsy room is the primary room in this category. Unlike almost every other space in the station, it is very much a closed space, with small windows only in its doors. Here, under a clearly impractical but suitably expressionistic lighting scheme, bodies are cleaned, examined, and (if need be) taken apart in autopsies performed by Dr. Albert "Doc" Robbins, and his assistant David Phillips, and observed variously by Grissom and others. In these scenes, the body itself is reconfigured as evidence, literally taken apart with scalpels, saws and other tools, as well as figuratively dismantled via editing and special effects. Robbins is the primary storyteller in this space (he is rarely seen anywhere else), and his autopsies are the final word on the victim's cause of death, vividly depicting the effects of, for example, a wooden stake through the head (3.16), a brutal beating (4.18), or, in the morbidly comic 7.21, a conjunction of multiple, unlikely injuries including faked snake bites, an allergic reaction to shrimp, and a perforated trachea.

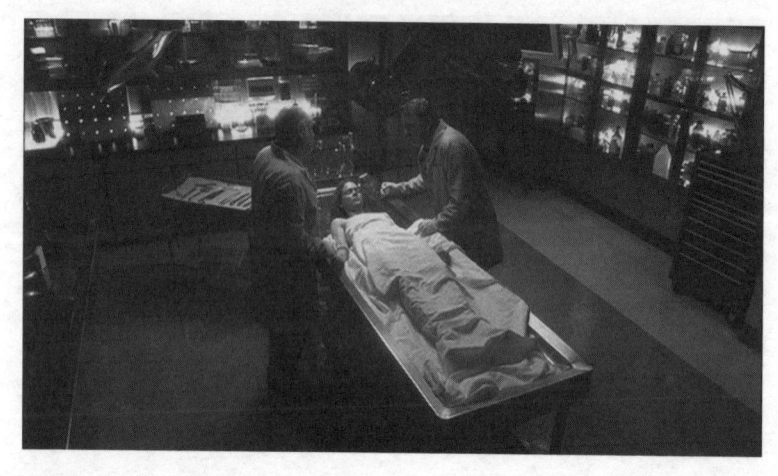

The autopsy room: Grissom and Doc Robbins diagnose the cause of death (COD), in 3.21 "Forever."

While the labs are the domain of physical science, the interrogation room, a more standard part of TV crime drama, is the stage for the ultimate psychological drama of accusation, denial, and eventual resolution (whether as confession or submission). "The box" on *Homicide: Life on the Street* (NBC, 1993–9) is arguably the genre's most stylized incarnation, but *CSI*'s room takes on a similar prominence in its narratives. Like most spaces in the LVPD station, the room is visible to external scrutiny, with windows to the hall as well as the standard one-way glass to the adjoining observation room. It is also the primary domain of the series' most prominent police officer, Detective Jim Brass. While the criminalists work on evidence gathered in the field and processed in the labs through microscopes, computers, and chemicals, Brass, as a typical TV cop, works directly on people, with his eyes and his voice. However, the general emphasis on spectacle persists in these scenes: it is Brass' observations of the suspects' reactions to his provocations that determine his course of action in the interrogations. Typically, Brass goes straight to the suspects' insecurities, often humiliating them by insinuating their guilt or mocking their attempted alibis with a sardonic "Yeah, sure. I understand." Brass is also often

The interrogation room: Catherine and Brass confront the suspicious parents of a dead child, in 4.4 "Feeling The Heat."

accompanied in the room by one or more CSIs, who produce and describe incriminating evidence, backing up his fiery accusations with the trump card of science.

However, this is still a show in which scientists are the heroes, and the detectives are secondary. Accordingly, and controversially, in a clean break with established police procedure, the CSIs are often the ones driving the questions both in the field and in the interrogation room, their scientific authority adding weight to the moral outrage they can express as accusers. In these scenes, the criminalists' particular personality traits come to the fore, after having been suppressed during their investigations. Sara's seething rage at cruelty, Catherine's disgust at negligent parents, and Nick's sympathetic demeanor all typically emerge when confronting criminals. In stark contrast, Grissom typically treats each such exchange as an intellectual encounter, coolly probing serial killers in 2.13, 5.6 and 7.24, and patiently prodding answers from the cannibalistic fitness devotee in 1.21, the murderous teen science whiz in 3.17, the lonely physician in 4.12 (an otherwise kindred soul), and the apologetic former sex offender in 7.6.

Revelation

The investigation comes to a head once all the seeming pieces of evidence point only to one possible cause. At that point, the stage is set for the final confrontation with the primary suspect(s), and the ultimate revelation of their guilt. While this is often a heavily-fraught and ambivalent moment in reality (since evidence rarely points as cleanly and directly to one guilty party), on *CSI* it is clearly a culminating moment, as the criminalists detail the evidence, and suspects realize they've been caught. Once formally confronted with these crucial bits of evidence, suspects are then usually formally arrested, though all subsequent events (arraignment, trial, sentencing, etc.) are almost never referred to in the narrative. The crime lab's job is to gather and process enough evidence to convince the Clark County DA's office to press criminal charges; what happens at that point is beyond their control, and beyond the narrative interest of the series. All that matters narratively is that the evidence is pinned to particular suspects, and they are revealed as the killers. However, on rare occasions, as in 2.2, 3.6, 4.12, and most of the season seven "Miniature Killer" storyline, the team's investigations do not produce enough evidence to press any charges, leaving the crimes, and their social disruptions, unresolved.

Getting to that precise point, culminating the long investigation with a confession or certain arraignment, is inevitably represented in a tense scene, that almost always takes place in the interrogation room. The team walks the suspects, usually with their lawyers present, through the evidence, particularly indicating elements that were difficult to prove. This admission reinforces their credibility as investigators, essentially saying to the suspect "you might have had us there, but we found you out anyway." Typically this scene is the dramatic high point of each episode, the one moment where our protagonists face off openly with proven (by their standards, at least) criminals. This is another convention taken completely from classic detective fiction, and particularly the novels of Agatha Christie, as the sleuth tells how they solved the mystery and identifies the killer. Their reactions to the criminal's realizations that they have been caught are meant to mirror ours'; we are disgusted at the killers, but pleased that they have been apprehended.

Some revelation scenes offer a different spin on this moment, however, "revealing" matters more compelling than just the identity of the killer. For example, Ashley, the teen girl in 4.10, shocks Sara with her admission that she used a phony rape allegation to lure conspirators to the murder of a teen boy for only a few hundred dollars, and her confidence of her acquittal because she "dresses up real nice. Couple barettes, little lace collar, two dead parents. I'll be the saddest little girl in the world."[8] Similarly, in 2.20, even Grissom is rendered speechless following the confession from two young girls that they killed the neighborhood "cat lady" only because they wanted one of her cats. In 1.9, the team reacts with dismay upon learning that none of the people they'd proven responsible for the death of a belligerent airplane passenger will be prosecuted.

Gathering the Evidence

CSI episodes routinely trace this narrative path, establishing crimes, following investigations, and revealing criminals with verve and panache. They consistently deliver just what they set out to do, and keep us transfixed by spectacular science and the time-honored traditions of detective fiction. The scene of their crimes, Las Vegas, is a critical component of the series' success in this regard, and its multiple incarnations on *CSI* are the subject of the next chapter.

Chapter 2

What Happens in *CSI*'s Vegas

I don't know what city you live in, Missy, but in Las Vegas, unusual is what happens when you leave the house.
(Handbill guy, 2.8, "Slaves of Las Vegas")[1]

Setting is a crucial, if underappreciated, part of television storytelling. The locations used or implied in a series shape its characters, actions, and narrative possibilities, no matter how mundane (a suburban home) or fantastic (a spaceship). Still, the standard locations of television narrative – hospitals, law firms, urban apartments, etc. – are typically used broadly, offering only minimal guidelines to our understanding of how the series' world works. They sacrifice specificity for stereotype, presenting settings that, while they may technically be located in specific places, function more often as mere generic backdrops. However, most crime dramas, following a model established by *Dragnet*'s distinctive early use of Los Angeles in the 1950s, have foregrounded their locales as particular sites of corruption, violence, excitement, desperation, heroism, and people's workaday lives. *Hawaii Five-O*'s Honolulu (CBS, 1968–80), *Law & Order*'s New York (NBC, 1990–), *Miami Vice*'s Miami (NBC, 1984–9), *Saving Grace*'s Oklahoma City (TNT, 2007–10), *The Shield*'s Los Angeles (FX, 2002–8), and *The Wire*'s Baltimore (HBO, 2004–8) are a few of the many iconic examples of how specific urban settings have been used to add a richer texture to the kinds of stories crime series can tell, and the kinds of places they show. Cities become critical features of these series, shaping our expectations of possible events, people, and sensibilities.

Even *Hill Street Blues*' unnamed but vaguely "rust belt" city (actually Southern California studio backdrops and redressed buildings/streets) evocatively functioned in this way for its loyal viewers over its six-year run in the 1980s.

Each of the three *CSI* series exploits its setting in this fashion; two even announce their cities in their titles, raising the expectations of specificity. As with the spinoffs' use of Miami and New York, Las Vegas is integral to the original *CSI*. While Las Vegas is not one of the nation's largest cities, its rapid development as a major resort destination and its subsequent busts and booms have made it one of the most iconic and distinctive places in post-World War II America. As many urban historians and cultural critics have examined, its particular mix of extreme environment, illicit power, rapid growth, and consumerist fantasy secured its unique place in the twentieth century American cultural imaginary, and has largely fueled its continuing status thus far in the twenty-first century.[2] Media critic Neil Postman famously stated in his polemical *Amusing Ourselves To Death* that, whereas the political and industrial spirits of Boston, New York, and Chicago dominated previous eras in American history, the urban standard bearer of the late-twentieth century was Las Vegas: "Las Vegas is a city entirely devoted to the idea of entertainment, and as such proclaims the spirit of a culture in which all public discourse increasingly takes the form of entertainment" (1985: 3). It is not surprising that most media representations of the city – from the original *Ocean's 11* (1960) to the raunchy comedy *The Hangover* (2009), as well as many television sitcoms and reality series – have focused exclusively on this, most media-friendly vision of Las Vegas. The city is typically shown in advertising, film, and television as a gaudy playground of casinos, nightclubs, and hotel suites, a place seemingly existing only for tourist indulgence, where everybody visits, but nobody "really" lives. At the other extreme, as seen less frequently, in films like *Lost in America* (1985), *Casino* (1995), and *Leaving Las Vegas* (1995), the city is portrayed as the ultimate incarnation of banal American indulgence, where a well-oiled pleasure industry fleeces awestruck tourists, and the last vestiges of normative social behavior are stripped away.

Though it certainly draws from these well-established conventions of Vegas-as-paradise and Vegas-as-hell, *CSI* also broadens this palette considerably by treating Las Vegas as a dynamic, diverse city, rather than only as a resort or sleaze pit. While the casinos, lights, and illicit thrills – and the millions of visitors that they draw – are certainly the primary economic and cultural fact of life there, Las Vegas is also home to nearly 2 million highly varied people. Like people everywhere, Las Vegans work, laugh, cry, suffer, have dreams, have fears, pay taxes, raise families, and try to stay afloat. Like any similarly-sized city, Las Vegas also has its share of crime, much of it unrelated to the casinos, hotels, and nightclubs. This chapter examines *CSI*'s varied representations of Las Vegas, which draw from and produce four distinct visions of the city and its people.

The Four Vegases

Although *CSI* is primarily shot in studios and locations near Santa Clarita, California (about 280 miles southwest of the Strip), its producers strive for verisimilitude, that is, to accurately represent a Las Vegas atmosphere and sensibility. As with most films and television shows, this need not entail actually shooting in the setting depicted: the conventions of cinematic realism have consistently allowed for approximations, even in works relying extensively on specific settings. Thus, in *CSI*, Southern California hills, deserts, neighborhoods, office buildings, and even casinos – which thrive by being several hours closer to millions of potential gamblers than those in Nevada – most often stand in for their Vegas counterparts. However, despite rarely shooting there, the series is narratively grounded in Nevada. In most episodes, a handful of aerial shots of the Strip are all that is needed to remind viewers of Las Vegas. However, the series consistently represents Vegas beyond this, generally opting to draw from real occupations (e.g., casino pit boss, dancer, blackjack dealer, etc.), policing practices, argot (e.g., referring to busy east-west thoroughfare Tropicana Avenue as "Trop"), and people, as well as occasionally actually shooting there. For example, longtime local news anchor Paula Francis has reenacted her job, as herself, many times on the series, reporting fake news stories relating to the cases at hand.

Similarly, colorful multiple-term Las Vegas mayor Oscar Goodman, himself a famous mob defense lawyer, played a high-powered criminal defense lawyer for a wealthy client in 4.14. In 5.24, Tony Curtis and Frank Gorshin (in his last screen role) even played themselves in a brief cameo (as over-the-hill cavorting Vegas celebrities).

When it does shoot in Las Vegas, *CSI* goes for maximum visual appeal, utilizing highly-recognizable spots and vistas, ranging from the Bellagio fountain to the Neon Boneyard east of downtown. Significantly, although the series often utilizes a few fictional stand-in resorts to bear the brunt of its Strip-inspired crimes (e.g., the Rampart, the Palermo, the Tangiers), it has also staged deaths at actual Vegas landmarks, including the Palms (seasons three and four), and, most extensively, the Cirque du Soleil show *Ka* (staged at the MGM Grand Hotel), where a woman was crushed to death by a moving platform in 7.1. These moments are relatively rare, but they do not need to be frequent; the occasional appearance of the cast at a real Vegas landmark is enough to bolster the overall verisimilitude of the series' otherwise fabricated Las Vegas. These effectual product placements indicate how *CSI*'s Vegas, while presented as deadly, is also rendered as normative, as a place one could actually visit.

These explicitly local references enhance the four visions of Las Vegas generally deployed in *CSI*. Each reinforces the others, and collectively they assert the central authority of the CSI team as the only characters effectively able to understand and move through all of these spaces. Las Vegas itself is, in other words, part of the evidence under investigation. The remaining sections of this chapter trace how *CSI* uses these dimensions to explore and expand its representations of Las Vegas. First, and most prominently, is the stereotypical Las Vegas of twenty-first-century popular imagination: the "Sin City" of unabashed luxury and decadence visited by over 37 million people in 2008.[3] This is the Las Vegas dominated by fantasy, where Americans (and much of the world) come to indulge in state-of-the-art luxury and entertainment. As seen in *CSI*, this Vegas is also a high-tech, high-security machine dedicated to the production of the illusion of such fantasies. Behind this lies the Las Vegas of its actual inhabitants: the dynamic, explosively-built city they work and make their lives in. Most of the victims and criminals on *CSI*

The Strip, in nocturnal glory, in 5.1 "Viva Las Vegas."

inhabit this "workaday" Vegas, where the Strip is mostly regarded as a large factory in a company town. Of course, both of these visions of contemporary Las Vegas are figuratively and literally built upon the foundations of "Old Vegas": the glitzy, neon-drenched and mob-dominated adult playground of the 1950s through 1970s. On *CSI*, this is the Vegas of colorful legends and ghosts, against which the contemporary city – and its people – are rendered both more sophisticated and less vibrant. Last, there are the spaces that surround and, through contrast, help enhance the audacity of Las Vegas: the wilderness, ranches, and remote small towns of Nevada. As is common in crime fiction set in the American west, the deserts and mountains surrounding Las Vegas represent the borders of civilization, where human law ultimately falls away.

Sin City

While the boundary between "old" and "new" Vegas is as indeterminate as any historical transition, long-time Las Vegans can pin it down to November 22, 1989. On that date, developer Steve Wynn's gargantuan

Mirage resort opened its doors on the Strip. By far the largest hotel in town at that point, the Mirage ushered in a new era of megadevelopment, premised not only on gambling, or even on "gaming," the new softer euphemism, but on "entertainment" more broadly. After all, with casinos beginning to open across the country at that time, Las Vegas could no longer rely on the singular or even primary appeal of blackjack and slots to lure visitors to its remote desert location. With its tropical-themed design – complete with indoor rain forest and erupting volcano – and top-notch amenities, the Mirage sought to recreate the original postwar sensation of "exotic" Las Vegas for a new generation of visitors. The success and notoriety of the hotel helped recharge development, and Las Vegas ratcheted up the scale of its ambition, eventually reclaiming its throne as the ultimate American resort destination. Along the way, the entire geography of the Strip – and the surrounding valley – was transformed in the 1990s and 2000s, as the aging façades of old Las Vegas were imploded to make way for a new regime of architectural hyperbole and monumental pleasures. Today, the gaudy attractions of the Strip – not only hotels and casinos, but world-class dining, shopping, live entertainment, nightclubs, thrill rides, and other diversions – are, effectively, the totality of Las Vegas for most people who experience it vicariously in the media, and even for most of the tens of millions who visit it every year. The Strip is the most prominent visual feature in Las Vegas, as emblematic as New York's skyline or Los Angeles' hills. As a testament to its iconic status in global culture in the early twenty-first century, it dominates the opening shots of nearly all *CSI* episodes, from the towering Stratosphere at its top, to the ostentatious faux-Europe in its middle, and the Disneyesque pyramid, castle, and miniature Manhattan on its southern end.

Moreover, though temporarily rebranded as a colorful "family" attraction in the early 1990s, Vegas had regained its status as America's premier adult playground by the early 2000s, on the heels of sumptuous high-end resorts like the Bellagio, Venetian, Paris, Palms, and Mandalay Bay. At that time, the powerful Las Vegas Convention and Visitors Authority (LVCVA) debuted the slogan "what happens in Vegas, stays in Vegas," promoting a prevailing attitude of indulging in otherwise "forbidden" pleasures as part of the area's urban branding.[4] Such a slogan is apposite for the Strip as seen on *CSI*: the luxuriant center of hegemonic indulgence, an intoxicating and potentially dangerous libertine space, where dazzled visitors (often, stereotypically, from the Midwest) often lose their bearings and presume that there are no consequences. Local historian Hal Rothman notes that what "Las Vegas does better than any place else on the planet is plane off the rough edges of a visitor's experience and make the traveler, however ordinary, the center of the story ... it can always be whatever you want it to be as long as you're willing to pay for it" (2003: 33–34).

When the Strip is the crime scene, it is generally conveyed knowingly, in broad, theatrical notes that dramatize both the allure and dangers of Sin City. *CSI* often reminds its tourist victims – and tourist criminals – that the consequences of their actions will stay with them long after they leave Vegas (if indeed they live long enough to leave). Thus, while the criminalists and other locals always regard the attractions of the Strip in a matter-of-fact way, the fates of visitors are often the result of their inability to manage themselves in this space. "You remember the MGM fire?," Grissom asks Detective Lockwood in 3.16. "We found people burned to their slot machines 'cause they wouldn't leave the action."[5] In these stories, the Strip functions as an enticing spark to the familiar crime-story motivators of avarice, lust, envy, and wrath, where stereotypical out-of-towners fall to its excesses. As Nick declares in 6.22, Vegas is essentially a trap: "Nothing here happens by chance. The odds are set before you get off the plane."[6] One of the earliest episodes (1.2) is a virtual template about the price the Strip exacts, as the winner of a huge slot machine jackpot is thrown off a hotel roof by his jilted girlfriend.[7] Similarly, the main case in 1.14 entails a visiting wedding party covering up the murder of a male stripper, prompting Warrick to sternly remind the suspects that "laws don't end when you come to Vegas."[8] A visiting conventioneer is accused of murdering the prostitute who had "trick-rolled" him in 5.1 (though her death was eventually deemed accidental). In 4.1, a kinky local couple go on a killing spree, targeting visiting married couples looking to spice up their sex lives with the promise of a foursome; one of their near-victims justifies his actions by reiterating the LVCVA mantra: "[it] was Vegas. We were looking for a little excitement."[9] Even visiting cops are not immune

Death in Sin City: Grissom and Brass at another apparent murder in a Strip hotel, in 3.2 "The Accused Is Entitled."

from its influence, as seen in the murders occurring during a competitive large regional running race in 4.20.

In similar fashion, several episodes have focused on the abuse of privilege in Sin City, as visiting high-end suspects (usually celebrities) attempt to elude criminal investigations through their influence. In these stories, the infamous pleasures and costs of Sin City are magnified by economic and political power, with the CSIs put under greater pressures from their supervisors (i.e., Clark County politicians) and typically brazen high-rent TV lawyers. The burden of policing such a space is emphasized in drawn-out investigations and courtroom scenes. In 3.2, a young Hollywood star is put on trial for the murders of two prostitutes. In the media-driven trial, his legal defense team, including Grissom's old mentor Phillip Gerard, attempts unsuccessfully to discredit each criminalist, in part by citing their own connections to Sin City.[10] In 6.2, the team discovers that another young, hard-partying actor was the victim of autoerotic asphyxiation, and that his entourage had attempted to cover this up.

The methods and technologies of surveillance that are presented as essential to the series' criminal investigations are also explored in the functioning of the Sin City motif. *CSI* episodes regularly detail how almost nothing happens in a Strip resort outside the range of security cameras or personnel, or in connection to networked data systems. Time and again, as seen most extensively in 3.1, 4.1, 5.7, 6.2, and 7.3, the team – usually by way of their resident "computer geek" lab tech, Archie Johnson – retrace the movements of suspects and victims across casino floors, in hotel elevators, and into hotel rooms with surveillance video and other digital records (of movements, purchases, etc.). The implication is that the fantasy of freedom promoted by the very idea of Sin City actually comes with constant monitoring. The series, in keeping with contemporary assumptions about security, never undermines this ideology. Indeed, as indicated by its general focus on the production of visibility (as analyzed in the previous chapter), it implicitly argues that such technologies are integral to modern policing and modern urban living.

While the Strip is certainly the show's primary incarnation of Sin City, it is not the only famous Vegas locale explored. With its iconic "Vegas" features, Fremont Street, the hub of downtown Las Vegas (and, prior to the ascendancy of the Strip in the 1950s, the city's original center of casinos and hotels, famously described as "Glitter Gulch") has been used many times as a *CSI* location. Several blocks of the street were converted to a walking mall in the mid-1990s, dominated by a gaudy overhead light show, the Fremont Street Experience. The ambience of cheap kitsch and old-school gambling (no "gaming" here) in aging hotels, casinos, and gift shops was retained in the refit, but was now visually embellished by the endlessly pulsating light show, and the accompanying foot traffic that now typically saunters (and staggers) through the area. While there is no shortage of lower-end experiences on the Strip itself (as any half-hour walk up the east side of the street between Tropicana and Sands will demonstrate), they are dwarfed there by the monumental scale of the opulent fantasies represented by the towering resorts. Downtown, the tawdry and down-and-out side of Las Vegas is much more dominant. Accordingly, *CSI* has productively used Fremont Street to play up both the fantasy and tragic reality of contemporary Vegas. In 5.1, its old-school casino lights mock the bottomed-out desperation of both the unlucky gambler and the young hot-dog cart attendant who eventually kills him.[11] In 6.14, its low-rent hotels and dingy alleys provide the bleak setting for the vengeful killer's murders. In 7.24, Fremont Street's overhead light show serves as the surreal background to the Miniature Killer's attempted back-alley escape from her darkened apartment, and disorients her to the point of collapse in the crowd on the street.

Everyday Vegas

As chapter 1 described, crime drama always takes place against a backdrop of what is represented as normal life. Typically, fictional detectives will encounter people from all professions and social positions in their depicted work, ranging from corporate executives and politicians to drug dealers and prostitutes. *CSI* maintains this generic focus, but with the added factor of life and work specific to Las Vegas. However, despite the visual bracketing suggested by the aerial shots of hotels and casinos in nearly every episode, the actual plots of *CSI* rarely focus on visitors to the Strip. Most of the series' crimes and investigations occur in the "regular" parts of Vegas, and focus on locals. Beyond tourists, after all, Las Vegas is a busy, growing (if challenged in the late 2000s due to the collapse of the housing bubble and the global financial crisis) metro area of over 2 million people who live more or less like every other American. Despite the prominence of the Sin City motif in its promotion, and the constant visual reminders of the Strip in the series' transition shots, *CSI* actually depicts the work-a-day, "normal" Vegas far more often than the more lurid Sin City-themed, "only in Vegas" plots. As Rothman reminds us, "the new Las Vegas looks, talks, sounds, and acts like everywhere else." (2003: 146). Accordingly, the majority of plots on *CSI* deal with crimes that could happen virtually anywhere, affecting teachers, housewives, mechanics, real estate agents, supermarket clerks, doctors, the homeless, college students, industrial workers, CEOs, artists, and so on. In these stories, *CSI*'s Vegas functions as a more generic, less fantastic space, where "bad stuff happens" much as it would everywhere else. Doing so not only enables the series to use more potential crime narratives; it also expands the media representation of Las Vegas beyond the Sin City stereotype of a tourist's playground.

As Rothman also explains, however, many of these "regular" Las Vegans were lured to the city in the first place by the promises of opportunity and "reinvention" brought about by the area's explosive growth, which was prompted by the wave of resort development sparked by the Mirage in the late 1980s. The boom in resort development led to a boom in housing construction and local business development, which drew in hundreds of thousands of people from around the country and the world. In the wake of the industrial collapse and economic stagnation of the 1970s and 1980s, Las Vegas stood out as a massive engine of growth and possibility. The area's population doubled in the 1980s, and then doubled again in the 1990s. As Marc Cooper commented in his 2004 profile of Las Vegas, "at times over the last fifteen years, it was as if a great, invisible hand had gripped the North American continent and tilted it upward to stand on the corner of southern Nevada, sending everyone and anyone else not solidly anchored to a middle-class job tumbling headlong toward Vegas" (2004: 14). Indeed, as one of the very last bastions in America where a low-skill job (e.g., parking valet) could still drive a middle-class lifestyle, the attraction of Vegas was, and even still is, considerable. The region's promise of personal renewal is as intoxicating to the American cultural psyche as the allure of money and pleasure promised by the casinos and resorts. As Rothman notes, "Las Vegas is the court of last resort, the last place to start over, to reinvent yourself in the same way that the city does, time after time. For some it works, for some it doesn't, but they keep coming and trying" (2003: 142).

Alongside the prevalence of roles found all over America (if not the world), Las Vegas also offers everyday possibilities and dangers to its residents that are not generally found elsewhere (or at least not as legitimately). As Cooper argues, the historic mix of money, power and "sin" in Vegas has produced a wide array of workers of all socio-economic classes that cannot exist anywhere else (2004: 67–114). *CSI* explores these roles on occasion, focusing on, for example, a blackjack dealer single mother, and her teenage sons who became sportsbook runners (1.12); the deadly rivalries among magicians (3.5); exhausted pit bosses (4.23), multitasking exotic dancers (6.1), and transsexual showgirls (5.8). In almost every case, the criminalists take these people and professions in their stride, understanding that no matter how unusual their jobs may seem to the outside world, they are integral parts of the everyday fabric of Vegas. According to Cohan, *CSI*'s "Las Vegas is a twenty-first-century metropolis with a cultural ethos all its own that leaves a distinctive imprint upon the lives of those who live and work there" (2008: 105).

Along those lines, the series has often explored this issue of what effects Las Vegas has on its children, who take its differences for granted. Significantly, while the series still functions in part as a promotional vehicle for Las Vegas overall, it also asserts a normative American moralizing tone, suggesting that the proximity to Sin City corrodes innocence. Catherine's daughter Lindsey is the primary cipher for these tensions throughout the series. Although she is rarely seen, her mentions and appearances are always folded into single-mom Catherine's worries and self-imposed guilt about attempting to raise a daughter in Vegas. As early as the pilot (1.1), Catherine is shown assuaging her fears for Lindsey's safety when, shaken from having to question a young girl about a possible sexual assault, she rushes home to check on Lindsey sleeping in bed. Catherine's back story as an exotic dancer who "escaped" that world for the more legitimate arena of criminal investigation uncertainly validates and opposes the Vegas career model. As the next chapter will explore, while her dancing experiences gives her a greater ability to assess people (particularly men), and a deep respect for Vegas' working entertainers (particularly women), she nonetheless is determined to keep her daughter from following that path.[12] In 5.3, after police catch Lindsey trying to hitch a ride on Fremont Street, Catherine asks her "what's next?"; Lindsey replies "stripping." Although she tells Grissom that she does not want Lindsey "to be this frightened, paranoid kid," later in the episode Catherine attempts to scare Lindsey into obedience by showing her the body of a dead female runaway in the morgue, much to Doc Robbins' dismay and anger.[13] In 7.2, Lindsey is even kidnapped in the plot to extort money from her wealthy grandfather, casino magnate Sam Braun. Parents and children alike in the series regularly express how difficult it is to stay conscientious while living in Sin City's shadow. As Sandra Hillman, the bereaved blackjack dealer in 1.12 who's apparently lost one son to an armed robbery, and is trying to get her other son out of "running" sports bets, states, "We've had full-scale wars about him doing that – carrying around that kind of money – but does he stop? No."[14]

In 5.7, one high school girl goes missing and another is found dead in a Strip hotel suite, following a party thrown by elite high school kids. The incident prompts the kids (rich and poor alike) to blame Vegas itself for their corruption. As one student, Dean Tate, tells Brass, "You don't understand what it's like to be born and raised here. . . . it's lucky that I'm not a drug dealer, and Mr. Mack [the wealthy father of the missing girl] should be happy Janelle's not a junkie stripper."[15] Two seasons later, 7.4 offered the series' most spectacularly damning (if also breathlessly moralizing) argument against raising children in Las Vegas, suggesting that they'd likely become amoral monsters. In the episode, tourists and workers (and Greg, in the midst of rescuing one victim) are brutally beaten by gangs of masked teens, who are eventually found to be bored locals looking for thrills. At the close of the episode, as the team ruminates on how such random violence could happen, Grissom, in a particularly strident moment of sermonizing, notes that "our culture preaches that you shouldn't be ashamed of anything you do any more. And unfortunately, this city is built on the principle that there's no such thing as guilt."[16]

Old Vegas

Old Las Vegas functions as both myth and history on *CSI*. As myth, it allows the series to draw upon the Vegas most deep-seated in American popular memory: the glitzy, mob-managed adult mecca of the 1950s to 1970s, where the Rat Pack, Elvis, Howard Hughes, and scores of legitimated gangsters roamed the casinos of the new neon-draped Strip, and middle-America first learned to indulge in its illicit desires. As history, *CSI*'s construction of Old Vegas places these events and figures of myth into real social and political contexts, and even attempts to demythologize certain aspects, as real events, places, and people in Vegas history are often brought up indirectly, and occasionally by name.

For example, the brief history of Las Vegas' first desegregated hotel/casino, the Moulin Rouge, which was only open for six months in 1955, was represented in 9.8 as a story of doomed interracial lovers and a racist justice system in the fictional La Chateau Rouge. The team solves a willfully mishandled murder from 50 years before, with Grissom himself confronting the retired cop who oversaw the original case. The tragedy of the 1950s affair between a white woman and a black man was contrasted with the now unremarkable interracial romance of two young would-be pop stars (appearing in a fictionalized knock-off of *American Idol* called *Overnight Sensation*). In this episode, as with most of those "remembering" Old Vegas, present-day Vegas is figured as both more enlightened yet somehow less vital than the past. That is, though Old Vegas is figuratively filled with injustices typically associated with the times (e.g., racism and sexism) that our sophisticated twenty-first century criminalists can right, the past is also lamented as an unfairly discarded part of Vegas' identity. "The other great cities – New York, Chicago, London – they restored," notes Tony Mumms, the ostensible curator of the Liberace Museum in 1.15, "But in this town, they destroy."[17]

At other times, the series wallows in a romantic notion of Old Vegas as the playground of powerful crime lords and Hollywood stars. Two episodes stand out in this regard, each both lamenting the memory of this version of Old Vegas, and reiterating the greater moral authority of "our" contemporary Vegas. In 6.13, Faye Dunaway plays Lois O'Neill, a retired showgirl, a popular party hostess and one-time mistress of a powerful mob figure who is about to release a "tell-all" book about her memories of the mob in Old Vegas. Hiding her cancer, she sets up her death (an assisted suicide at the hands of one her lover's former enforcers) to make it look like an old-style mob hit. The episode opens with old film footage of the Strip and Glitter Gulch circa 1960, and closes with Frank Sinatra singing, as direct a reference to Old Vegas as possible. The case, and O'Neill's book, inspires Greg to do his own research for a book on Vegas gangsters, which becomes a

Sam Braun, icon of Old Vegas, keeping secrets from Catherine, in 3.23 "Inside The Box."

running plot point for the next two years. Episode 7.9 takes an even more theatrical look at Old Vegas, featuring the elusive and long-thought-dead 1970s mob boss Mickey Dunn (played by Roger Daltrey, the lead singer of the Who, the band responsible for *CSI*'s title song "Who Are You?") who, sensing he's near the end of his life, returns from hiding to exact revenge on the members of his crew who double-crossed him in 1976. The episode is clearly inspired by the film *Casino*, as it features several seventies pop songs and flashbacks (including a glimpse at a teenage Catherine Willows, who admits to having a crush on Dunn at the time). Here, while Old Vegas is clearly meant to be "the stuff of legend" – the episode's title is "Living Legend" – it is also figured as a virtually lawless time where the mob ruled and the police were corrupt or ineffective. Warrick comments that "there were a lot of dirty cops back then," to which Catherine replies, "there was a lot of dirty everything back then."[18]

The most prominent incarnation of the myth and history of Old Vegas in the series is the character of Sam Braun (played in seasons two through seven by Scott Wilson). Braun is an amalgam of the archetypal old and new Vegas, a one-time mob enforcer turned casino and real estate magnate. His position at the center of the series' Old Vegas mythology is cemented by the startling revelation in 3.23 that he is actually Catherine Willows' father. As a character, Braun draws on the shady mythos of such iconic Old Vegas figures as Benny Binion, Moe Dalitz, and Frank "Lefty" Rosenthal, but also on the entrepreneurial foresight associated with the quintessential "father" of the new Vegas, developer Steve Wynn. While Braun's past and present culpability in criminal actions is rendered ambiguous in the series as a whole (despite heavy suggestions that he was a feared and lethal figure in the 1960s and 1970s), his narrative presence as the primary physical link to the storied past gives the series an ongoing foothold in the Old Vegas mythos. Braun's stature in this regard even extends beyond his presence. He is mentioned, though not seen, in several episodes as having "run" old Vegas, as in 3.16, when, upon seeing an old mechanical slot machine, Nick asks Grissom when he last saw "a dinosaur like this," and Grissom replies "not since Sam Braun ran the town."[19] Braun's spectacular death under a casino façade in 7.2, shot, rather appropriately, by an irate former business partner, marks the end of his physical presence, but certainly not the end of his legacy, as his estate, affairs, and reputation are now entrusted to his sole remaining heir, Catherine.

The wilderness

Las Vegas sits in a low desert valley surrounded by rugged mountain ranges and a large concentration of Federally-owned land. Some of the remotest wilderness in the continental United States lies less than 2 hours' drive from the Strip, in any direction. The Las Vegas Metropolitan Police Department, whose jurisdiction extends over most of Clark County (i.e., the southeastern tip of Nevada), must also handle cases in much of these areas, far removed from the city. *CSI* replicates this real-life policing, and effectively uses the wilderness (which, for the sake of most narratives, also includes small-town Nevada) as a counterpoint to its usual urban focus.

While *CSI* occasionally investigates crimes at higher elevations, in Clark County's mountains (e.g., in 2.12, 2.21, and 5.14), the wilderness is primarily depicted in the series through the Mojave Desert, the vast,

Death in the Wilderness: Grissom, Catherine, and Brass at a triple murder scene in the Mojave Desert, in 3.23 "Inside The Box."

inhospitable land stretching south from Nevada into Arizona and California. As iconic as the Strip, the desert here is used as it has long been used in Vegas-set crime fiction (and legend): as the last stop, the end of civilization, that is, where one goes (or is taken) to die. Away from the comforts of the city, and exposed to the full brunt of nature, humanity is typically altered in this space. Here, the wilderness can foster monsters, as in the serial killers caught in 1.11 and 4.8, or, more typically, madness, as in 4.18's enraged killer, 5.25's distraught father, 6.4's UFO cult, or 6.15's neo-Nazi doctor. It is also an evocative setting for mortal dramas, like teen suicides (3.21), double crosses (3.23), dog-fighting rings (8.10), or the Miniature Killer's elaborately theatrical kidnapping and attempted murder of Sara Sidle (7.24–8.1). The desert is typically shot in ways to emphasize its isolation and extreme environment, with telephoto shots to enhance the heat waves, and color grading and lens flare to suggest intense heat and light. The extended searches for the model's body in 4.8, for the cult in 6.4, and for Sara in 8.1, exemplify this augmented use of the desert – as a place of near hopelessness and isolation, where civilization fails to protect people from more fundamental realities.

Death in the Wilderness: Grissom studies a headless body buried up to its shoulders in a remote forest, in 4.6 "Jackpot."

Small-town Nevada also effectively functions as "wilderness" in *CSI*, in the sense that the team's "city" methods do not function as reliably as they are used to when they are in these environments. Justice here is rendered in much starker, black-and-white terms than in Las Vegas, challenging the team's ability to function beyond the city. This was seen most explicitly in 4.6, when Grissom travels alone outside their usual jurisdiction, to the northern Nevada mountain town of Jackpot, to assist in an unusual murder with Las Vegas connections. Throughout the episode, the locals regard Grissom as the stereotypical stranger, with suspicion or derision for his methodical techniques. Threatened several times, Grissom refuses to back down, and even calmly assembles a makeshift field kit out of materials found at the tiny local hardware store, after his own kit is stolen. The crime is eventually revealed to be one of passion, as a local teen became incensed that his father engaged in a sexual relationship with his (the teen's) college roommate, and murders the latter, leaving his body, half-buried, deep in the woods. In this case, the evidence ultimately "reveals" the man's homosexuality, which he is desperate to keep a secret, under the normative rules of small-town America. Grissom, here the enlightened, liberal urban sophisticate, is saddened by the bigotry that prompted the murder. In 6.5, most of the team wrestles with the limited resources of small-town law enforcement in the case of a murdered family; Warrick mutters "it's a joke," when forced to use a microscope from a high school science lab. In 7.11, Catherine and Nick confront a small-town sheriff over a coerced confession made in a rushed judgment, which sent an unpleasant man (and previous killer) to jail, but left the actual murderer free. The sheriff cites the demand for justice, and defends her decision since the convicted killer, Guffey, was also a deadly criminal. Catherine, again functioning as the more enlightened "city" cop, is appalled at that reasoning; she and Nick reopen the case, eventually locating the actual killer.

Crime Scenes

Las Vegas is an essential component of *CSI*. Its familiarity to viewers, through decades of media exposure and tourism, and unique place in the American imaginary make it a particularly suitable setting for popular television drama. Likewise, the component sensibilities of Vegas explored here – as indulgent resort, as workaday city, as mythic realm, and as environmental extreme – set the stage for a wide of variety of compelling, horrific, and spectacular crimes, which our protagonists are uniquely qualified to solve.

That said, however central it is to the series' sensibility, Las Vegas is not what ultimately propels *CSI* season after season; the regular characters do. The next chapter explores their contributions.

Chapter 3

Finding Balance
Professionalism in Serial Narrative

> CATHERINE: I went out after work. Is it a crime to want a little human contact?
> GRISSOM: I guess that's why I don't go out. (5.22, "Weeping Willows")[1]

As I argued in chapter 1, procedure drives spectacle and narrative in much television drama, and particularly in the *CSI* series. A "professional" – i.e., one trained and even officially certified in particular, socially-sanctioned tasks and responsibilities – must display certain skills and attitudes which prove their credibility. TV's procedural dramas function as critical ideological sites where characters' professional attributes (and their shortcomings) are publicly displayed to other characters, as well as to viewers at home.[2] These professional competencies and ethics help ground the drama at the point of the individual in terms readily accessible in competitive social economies and enhance the very ideology of professionalism; for example, does Greg Sanders have "what it takes" to become a legitimate crime scene investigator? That said, even in a society as seemingly work- and assessment-obsessed as the United States, expectations of professionalism also demand that one have "a life" outside of one's career, which generally involves friends, family, material comforts, and domestic stability. Accordingly, in television procedural drama terms, a professional is someone who, while not perfect, is able to effectively (if not easily) balance the demands of her job and her personal life. Serial narratives centering on professionals are generally structured around how characters perform this balance over time.

Of course, the codes of professionalism typically depicted in television drama are generally limited both in terms of the kinds of careers (never only "jobs") portrayed, and the range of labor within those vocations. For the most part, even though representations in more recent years have included greater vulnerability, weakness, and even ugliness (e.g., *The Shield*'s Vic Mackey), television professionals typically embody normative, attractive societal ideals. We can only hope that cops are as driven as *Homicide*'s Frank Pembleton, doctors as dedicated as *ER*'s John Carter, or lawyers as indomitable as *Boston Legal*'s Alan Shore. Similarly, while we are typically led to identify with the victims, patients, and clients of TV professionals (i.e., as "regular" people in need of their expertise), we may also recognize our own behaviors and aspirations in them; for example, to want to have Alan Shore's wit and passion, but still sympathize with his personal demons. Even as limited popular representations, however, these roles are important in circulating codes and discourses of professionalism that still resonate with the broader culture. It is unlikely that procedural drama would have succeeded as a dominant television form if its characters and situations did not have some sort of emotional and intellectual resonance with viewers (and particularly among the upper middle-class viewers targeted by most prime time serial dramas). Thus, characters are expected to show compassion, technical competency, and occasionally brilliance, though not necessarily perfection.

Susanna Lee notes that crime drama has an important function of reassurance in the face of personal and social trauma, in that its protagonists, as idealized representatives of the justice system, are seen to be not only competent but dedicated professionals, despite the enormous difficulties they face in carrying out their jobs. "[TV crime drama] relies on this psychic tension between the inclination to (re)present violence and the inclination to moderate it with form and empathetic presence" (Lee 2004: 82). In other words, these procedural roles represent a larger idealized significance in modern society, suggesting that individuals can "make a difference," even in areas of life as seemingly defensive and futile as the modern legal or health care systems. While *CSI* certainly conveys this sense of dedicated professionalism and even social duty (as seen in particular in its pedagogical "show-and-tell" mode, described in the first chapter), as hybrid episodic-serial drama it probes more deeply than *Law & Order* by also tracing the impact these expectations of professionalism have on the protagonists both in the moment and over time. Each criminalist struggles with these expectations throughout the series, and faces lingering professional crises that challenge their abilities to continue.

Thus, while solving crimes is certainly its generic focus, *CSI*'s affective cultural function is subtler, yet broader: to explore human relationships, and particularly to model "professional balance" in modern life. Crime itself preceded the series, continues in the narrative in between the characters' shifts, and indeed will continue when the series ends. The CSI team cannot ultimately "solve" crime. What they can do, however, is apply their skills, practices, and ethics to the job at hand, not only decoding the evidence of specific crimes, but also discovering their own abilities and limits along the way. Accordingly, beyond merely demonstrating technical skills, the production of visibility on *CSI* also entails the representation of middle-class adulthood "professionalism." However, despite providing some insightful analyses of the series' presentation of criminology, most critics have elided or dismissed *CSI*'s characterizations. Martha Gever, for example, claims that the criminalists do not display "much of what is called an inner life" and that no "attempt is made to provide them with so-called well-rounded personalities" (2005: 454). While I agree that the characters are not particularly complex, I disagree that they have little "inner life." When it is approached as a serial, rather than only an episodic narrative, the series reveals the characters as not only competent professionals, but also struggling individuals. As Greg Smith wrote in his analysis of *Ally McBeal* (Fox, 1997–2002), analysis of serial dramas should look not only at plot, but at how plot illuminates character. We should look at "what plot events tell us about the interconnected world of the serial, how actions inflect our understanding of the dramatic community, and how the closed system of the serial sets up comparisons among characters" (2007: 73).

Generally eschewing ambiguity, popular television drama typically draws from a handful of primary emotional "colors" that are efficiently deployed by the production and easily understood by viewers. On

CSI, as with many crime dramas, the forces that the protagonists struggle to balance are predominantly represented as "logic" and "emotion." This binary has been used effectively for decades in all popular media, dramatizing modernity's longstanding head-heart split.[3] As examined in chapter 1, *CSI*'s conspicuous, if hyper-real, scientific ideology is arguably the most important part of its design, determining narrative possibilities and audiovisual style. This motif is also the key factor in its version of professionalism. Grissom, in particular, is presented as a model scientist: logical, meticulous, razor-sharp, deeply knowledgeable, insatiably curious, cool under pressure, sardonic, and generally affable, if occasionally abrupt. He leads by example and by explicit pedagogy. However, adhering to stereotypes of scientists, he is also often shown to be decidedly inept at personal relationships, and slow to acknowledge emotions – others' or even his own – in general. He is often awkwardly speechless at such moments. Meanwhile, his colleagues – Nick and Sara in particular – often err in the opposite manner, often letting their "hearts" hold sway over their "heads."[4] It is only in relatively rare moments of clarity (often following the processing of trauma) that the characters start to realize this imbalance, and take it upon themselves, with assistance from their friends, to effect change. Thus, despite its seeming machine-like precision, normative science, as displayed on *CSI*, is ideally a fully human endeavor, shaped by human actions and interpretations. Through the regular characters, science is shown to be frustrating (as with Grissom's anger at the investigation's inability to locate a body in 2.5), triumphant (as when Nick deduces a drowned woman had fallen from a higher altitude in 2.21), and absurd (as with Doc Robbins' scrapbook of celebrity deaths in Vegas). That said, on *CSI*, unlike more relationship-centric dramas like *ER* or even *The Closer*, moments of professional and personal reflection are relatively rare, and take a back seat to the investigations in most episodes. However, they are no less critical in the development of the characters over the course of episodes, entire seasons, or years.

Unlike film characters, who we only experience for a couple of hours, characters in serial television unfold over dozens of hours, and possibly years of episodes. In order to illustrate better how *CSI*'s serial storytelling has functioned to model normative adult professional life, the remainder of this chapter traces the biographies of its six main characters: Gil Grissom, Catherine Willows, Sara Sidle, Warrick Brown, Nick Stokes, and Greg Sanders. By comparison, the other regular and recurring characters who've appeared across the run of the show – Jim Brass, Albert Robbins, David Phillips, Sofia Curtis, David Hodges, and the various lab techs – have been relatively static, functioning primarily to advance the episodic narratives and assist the main cast. While they each have had their dramatic moments in the series (particularly Brass), they lack the overall serial progression the key regulars have displayed, and thus are not the focus here. Similarly, Raymond Langston (Laurence Fishburne), a middle-aged criminology professor who becomes a rookie CSI in season nine, replacing Grissom as a lead character, has not been on the series long enough to warrant much development beyond his initial biography. In order to effectively analyze serial narrative, particularly over such a long-running series, characters, and their changes over time, must be accounted for. The analyses that follow focus mostly on the key events and major qualities of each character that the series has conveyed over its run. It is important to note that these characters are always representations; choices made in production by cast and crew (and later by fan creativity) have also contributed to these characterizations.

Gil Grissom (William Petersen)

Supervising criminalist and lead character for *CSI*'s first eight and a half seasons, Gil Grissom is the clearest link back to earlier archetypal fictional sleuths, like Columbo, Hercule Poirot, and Sherlock Holmes. Grissom is a consummate detective, with fine-tuned observational skills and a rapid mind. He dives into each investigation with a sort of grim enthusiasm, challenging the other criminalists to keep up with him, and often boggling suspects and witnesses. He is a razor-sharp, virtually unflappable analyst while on cases, and a calm yet relentless interrogator when confronting suspects with evidence, only showing anger when his patience has been exhausted. However, unlike the usual generic detective, whose character is limited to their considerable skills, Grissom also has debilitating physical and psychological deficiencies and, over a great deal of time, learns to deal with them.[5]

Grissom's perpetual inability to connect to others, particularly intimately, is the defining feature of his emotional life. He has much in common with his sleuthing forebears and peers in this regard, men and women defined in large part by their considerable professional skills, which were often accompanied by lackluster interpersonal skills. While this emphasis on head over heart was not considered problematic in earlier detectives, it is represented in Grissom as a chronic imbalance. As a twenty-first century professional and team leader, he is expected to exhibit sympathy as well as intellect. Although he is represented as generally sociable, if a bit dry and brusque in everyday work interaction, he typically withdraws between tasks into silence and solitude rather than be around others, preferring to sit in his dark office, surrounded by books, biological samples, and insect collections. He is certainly fond and proud of his team, but he generally keeps them at arm's length, with the exception of Catherine, whom he respects greatly (even when they do not get along), in large part because she is not afraid to call him on his problems. As Catherine bluntly tells him in 1.17, "You're not good with people."[6] In 2.15, she reminds him that he needs to improve in that regard, if only because of his role as CSI supervisor: "You have responsibilities, and people are making a family around you whether you like it not, whether you give them permission or not."[7] The only women that seem to intrigue him are those that seemingly possess a temperament and intelligence similar to his own, including the recurring paleontologist Teri Miller (seasons one and three), the calm and methodical killer Susan Hillridge (in 1.21), and, most famously and intriguingly, the entrepreneurial dominatrix/philosopher Lady Heather (2.8, 3.15, 6.15, 7.23, 9.5), who is the first to pierce his façade. In a depiction unlikely to appear in a more traditional television treatment of this sexually-charged material, Grissom is represented as fascinated by her, and unquestioningly accepts the legitimacy of her work. She notes this acceptance, and quickly grows to understand him better than anyone else. In 2.8, she correctly surmises that "being known," is

Soulmates, or kindred intellects?: Grissom and Lady Heather get intimate, in 3.15 "Lady Heather's Box."

his greatest fear; in 3.15, when she is suspected in a murder (which she did not commit), she tells him "you fear me... because I've committed the one unforgivable act. I know you."[8]

While Lady Heather is the only character to really peer into his soul, Sara Sidle is figured as the only one to touch his heart. Their relationship functions as the primary emotional through-line of the series, the linchpin of its logic/emotion dichotomy. In keeping with his characterization as distant or detached, Grissom is presented as slow to acknowledge Sara's feelings for him, and even slower to acknowledge his own for her. Their awkward, years-long courtship played out not up front, as would be the case on most dramas, but in brief moments at work: a lingering glance, a faltering conversation, an occasional glimpse of candor. Along the way, Grissom's perpetual inability to communicate frustrates Sara and continually delays their eventual coupling. Grissom is shown tipping his hand at times in early seasons (e.g., letting her comfort him at an atypically frustrating moment in an investigation in 2.5; telling her she was especially beautiful in 2.16), but not knowing how to proceed. Sara even (unsuccessfully) asks him out to dinner in

Through one-way glass, Sara sees Grissom obliquely confess his feelings for her, in 4.12 "Butterflied."

3.22, warning him that "by the time you figure it out, you really could be too late." Grissom seems to have figured it out in the unusually meta-textual 4.12, dealing with a victim who bears an uncanny resemblance to Sara, and a middle-aged killer who is his emotional doppelganger. While he is unable to produce enough evidence to arraign this prime suspect, he recognizes himself, telling the killer in their final confrontation in the interrogation room (as, unknown to him, Sara looks on from the adjoining observation room; see figure) "It's sad, isn't it, doc? Guys like us. Couple of middle-aged men who've allowed their work to consume their lives. The only time we ever touch other people is when we're wearing our latex gloves. We wake up one day and realize that for fifty years we haven't really lived at all."[9] After another couple of years of this uncertainty, Grissom and Sara are finally revealed (though only to viewers; the rest of the team would only find out at the end of the following season) to be sleeping together in 6.24.

Grissom faces his own emotional uncertainty early on in the series' run, as his hearing begins to mysteriously deteriorate from the end of season one until he finally has surgery to save it at the end of season three. In between, his hearing occasionally, and unpredictably, simply stops working, leaving him embarrassed and frustrated. This was effectively conveyed in these scenes by presenting viewers with his audio perspective: increasingly muffled voices and even silence. Typically, Grissom kept this knowledge from the others, only confiding in Doc Robbins when he wants another opinion on his condition in 3.23, and, in the same episode, in Catherine, after she has figured it out for herself. In 3.2, his antagonistic former mentor, a Grissom-like figure with a keen sense of observation, tries to embarrass him on the witness stand by instructing a defense lawyer to speak softly so that Grissom can not hear her; he evades this tactic by reading her lips. Ultimately, as his hearing worsens over season three, he accepts his weakness and undergoes the surgery in 3.23, and has seemingly admitted his condition to the team by 4.1.

After this moment, Grissom's early impenetrable exterior starts to thaw a bit. While he could still be represented as generally circumspect and often defensive (as he is in season five, when his department nemesis, Conrad Ecklie, temporarily reassigns his team), he seems more willing to trust and open up to the others. He also becomes increasingly fatigued with his role, taking a leave of absence for a few months in season seven (actor William Petersen was taking time off from the series to perform in a play in Chicago) after several particularly frustrating and disturbing cases (including the apparent suicide of the man thought to be the Miniature Killer). While he is shown becoming closer to Sara after this, her near-death experience in the desert and subsequent sudden departure (in 8.7), and Warrick's murder (in 9.1) edges him to a tipping point. He announces his resignation to his team in 9.9 in typical, matter-of-fact style, without lead-up or ceremony, simply leaving at the end of 9.10. As Grissom tells Warrick in 2.4, he's a "ghost": "When I leave CSI, there won't be any cake in the break room. I'll just be gone."[10] In his last on-screen investigation, in the last few minutes of his final episode (9.10), he reunites with Sara at her Costa Rica research facility, fulfilling what Catherine had admonished him to do a year earlier (in 8.8), and finally following his heart rather than his head.[11]

Catherine Willows (Marg Helgenberger)

As the team's, and series', lead female, Catherine embodies many of the stereotypical traits associated with female cops in television crime fiction. However, she has also been one of the most intriguing characters in crime drama. It does not hurt, in this regard, that *CSI*'s showrunner is a woman (Carol Mendelsohn), that many of the series' key writers have been women, and that one of the franchise's primary criminalist technical advisers is a woman (Elizabeth Devine), each of them, alongside actor Marg Helgenberger, having built careers in notoriously male-dominated professions. Like most women of her generation, and the one before it, Catherine is represented as having had to fight for recognition and validation, though in not one but two overwhelmingly "masculine" fields, policing and science. In addition, her unique back story indicates that she had already had significant life and work experiences before the events depicted on the show. Raised alone in Vegas by a showgirl/cocktail waitress mother, Catherine was an exotic dancer in early adulthood, until becoming interested in police work after the murder of her best friend (as revealed in 2.17). Using money earned from her dancing, she then majored in medical science in college and eventually became a criminalist with the LVPD. Catherine is a single mother as well; she has a daughter, Lindsey (aged 18 by season 10), from a previous marriage to an irresponsible man (Eddie, who is killed in a car accident in 3.15). As the only parent on the team (Brass' daughter is an estranged adult), she often expresses frustration with her hours, pay, and support; it is her exhaustion that leads to the negligence (in not securing an unknown liquid in the lab) that causes the explosion in 3.22 that nearly kills Greg. Despite the frequent personal stress, however, she is also presented as arguably the most enthusiastic investigator on the team, and is rarely plagued by the sorts of self-doubt that sometimes hamper the younger CSIs. She possesses a confidence equal to Grissom's, but seems to take more pleasure in her work. As she tells Warrick in 4.7, "we don't just call these cases rush 'cause we're in a hurry. It's a rush 'cause our pulse races, it's a rush when we nail the guy."[12] However, Catherine's confidence is

Searching for "the rush": Catherine searching for an incriminating frame of film, in 3.8 "Snuff."

often shown to be vulnerable, as mistaken instincts, reckless decisions, and tragic events (such as the sudden, on-the-job assault at the crime scene in 3.4, and the kidnappings and murder in 7.1 and 7.2) challenge her ability to maintain balance.

In terms of professionalism, Catherine's primary function is to be the emotional "yang" to Grissom's logical "yin." Their depicted friendship and mutual respect models a "collective balance" in the professional workplace, though not without dramatic conflict over their differing methods of investigation. Thus, while Catherine's observational skills and attention to detail and procedure are shown to be almost as honed as Grissom's, she is also more likely to express her emotions on cases, and to follow her instincts at times, though that leads her astray as often as not. This is particularly the case in cases involving children, as she loses her cool with negligent or devious parents or other adults, as seen in 1.21, 3.5, 4.4, 4.21, 6.3, 6.6, and 8.13. Sometimes this passion even exceeds her professional boundaries and her better judgment, leading her to rash decisions. For example, in 1.21 she concocts a non-existent mandatory drug test in order to bring in a suspicious carny for questioning. In 8.13, her faulty suspicion of a minor sex offender (his one incident was almost 20 years in the past) in the death of a three-year-old girl is shown to ruin his life despite the fact that he was innocent of this crime. In 5.22, she hides the fact that she had had drinks and flirted with a man who became a prime suspect in a murder discovered later that night, until events force her to disclose this to an upset Grissom. Catherine is also occasionally impatient with Grissom's supervision, recognizing that he does not work with people as well as he does with evidence, as in 1.20, when she faked the deadline for a letter she needed him to write, because she knew he would not do the paperwork on time.

Over the course of the series, these aspects of Catherine's personality are developed, with sometimes tragic consequences. The most important event in this regard is the revelation, in 3.23, that Sam Braun, whom she had considered a fatherly, if emotionally distant, family friend, actually *is* her father. This revelation has immediate repercussions in season four, as both Catherine and Braun are shown adjusting to this new relationship, and dealing with the consequences of the manner in which it was discovered. Long suspecting Braun was her father, Catherine sneaks her own DNA into an analysis of a blood sample in the reopened investigation of the murder of Braun's lover several years before. The resultant evidence tampering – a common occurrence both in reality and on the series – is enough to derail the criminal case against Braun (in 4.1), and places Catherine's job in jeopardy. After this revelation, Catherine struggles to maintain her sense of integrity as Braun tries to improve their relationship. She's reluctant to accept money from him in season four, though she eventually does, for Lindsey's security. The relationship with her father turns deadly when she and Lindsey are brutally and consecutively kidnapped in 7.1 and 7.2 by a vengeful former business partner of Braun's, and he is eventually shot and killed in her arms in front of one of his hotels. Catherine's explicit connection with Braun (and with her showgirl mother and stripper past), makes her the series' most emblematic "Vegas" character: like the city itself, seeking legitimacy despite a history of sin and excess.

Catherine's gender and sexuality have also frequently been used as a source of narrative development. While her striking beauty – particularly while on the job – has prompted some criticism of the series' telegenic leads (particularly regarding what they wear to crime scenes), her looks actually have a narrative function in the context of the show. As a former stripper, Catherine is represented as in command of her body: she knows exactly how she looks and acts, and more importantly how others perceive her; she takes Lady Heather's remark (in 2.8) that she would "make a good dominatrix" as the compliment it is intended. Accordingly, she occasionally uses her sexuality as another tool in her kit, like dusting powder or a UV light, to help advance investigations. For example, in 7.11, she illicitly garners information from a prison inmate by slowly unbuttoning her blouse for each question he answers to her satisfaction. More directly, she defends her chess-like sexual manipulation of a dangerous suspect in a high-profile murder of a reality show contestant in 4.8 as a key part of the investigation, telling Sara (who is particularly upset about it), "I saw the look in Howard's eye. I used to make my living off that look. He wanted me. We needed him. I decided to exploit that situation. And as angry as that made you, when you're in my shoes, you'll do the same thing."[13] In addition, in a nod to persistent gender divisions, Catherine starts to become more self-conscious about her age, particularly given Vegas' youth-obsessed culture (which *CSI* often critiques, even while relying upon it for sex appeal). In 5.4, in a case involving plastic surgery, facial treatments, and a negligent doctor, Catherine is shown to be tempted by the promises of these products.

Like all the other characters, Catherine is also presented as having a difficult time finding stable relationships outside work. Indeed, the two serial romantic relationships she has on the series are with men she meets while working on cases; each ends after only a few episodes. In *CSI*'s usual close-to-the-vest style, a potential relationship with Warrick is hinted at in a handful of extended glances and possibly flirtatious exchanges, most notably in 5.2 and 5.16, lasting a total of a few dozen seconds of screen time, but enough to prompt her confession to him in 6.1 as she learns of his sudden marriage: "the thing that makes a fantasy great is the possibility that it might come true. And when you lose that possibility . . . it just kind of sucks."[14] Following

Fleeting connection: Catherine and Warrick share an (almost) intimate moment, helping fuel fan speculation about their unrequited passions, in 5.2 "Down The Drain."

through on this representation of unrequited desire, Catherine is shown breaking down and reacting more emotionally than the others upon the sight of Warrick's dead body in 9.1.

Like Grissom, Catherine is senior to the other CSIs, but regards herself more as a mentor than a teacher, reminding them that "Grissom's not always right," and that hard choices are sometimes necessary to the work at hand. As if to demonstrate this, in 4.8 she chooses Greg, who has only just started working in the field at that time, as her assistant investigator, despite loud protests from Nick and Sara, who are each more experienced. She argues, correctly, that Greg needs to work a case of this stature more than either of them. In season five, in the wake of Ecklie's dissolving of the original team, she becomes a shift supervisor, and has to toughen her relationships with Nick and Warrick in order to prove her mettle, telling them "I'm not Grissom. He let a lot of things slide that I won't."[15] In 7.12, she cuts off visiting criminalist Michael Keppler by admonishing him that he's a CSI and not a profiler, and that he should follow the evidence instead of his hunches. However, in the very next episode, she makes the "hard choice" to follow Keppler, as she's persuaded by him to strain ethical boundaries by faking a crime scene and investigation (including having to deceive her own team) in order to catch a killer.

Since losing her father, and coming to terms with her daughter's maturation, Catherine is shown to be gradually accepting leadership of the team in later seasons. In season nine, after Grissom's departure, she assumes the reins of the team, and is now the senior supervising CSI, though she still struggles with her confidence as a leader.

Sara Sidle (Jorja Fox)

Joining the team in the second episode, after the shocking murder of Holly Gribbs, Sara Sidle comes to the department having known Grissom as her teacher from several years before. This previous relationship would ultimately determine both characters' fates. Along the way, Sara struggles with her job. Presented as assertive and confident of her investigative abilities, she also has a short fuse, and lets some cases get under her skin. Accordingly, her largely unsuccessful struggle with professionalism is perhaps the most complex of any of the main characters'.

Early on, Sara, as an outsider, must work to gain the team's trust. She is disappointed at Grissom's quick reinstatement of Warrick (in 1.11), despite her filing a report on Warrick when she caught him gambling while on the clock. She is also often reminded by Grissom to keep her professional distance. He advises her in 1.16 that if she does not, each case will become "special, and then you'll burn out."[16] This advice proves to be prescient, on multiple occasions. However, by season two she also begins to realize that, like Grissom, she might be keeping too much bottled up, keeping a brave face when she needs to open up, and that perhaps she needs to resolve her feelings for him. In 2.12, she sees similarities between herself and the murder victim, a shy, lonely shut-in, and pledges to become more sociable. After that, though she has an ill-fated relationship with Hank Peddigrew (an EMT she met in 2.3) over most of season two and three, she accepts her attraction to Grissom, and gets more assertive in trying to get him to reciprocate.

Tenacity: Sara investigates every scrap of evidence at the scene of the accident, in 2.18 "Chasing the Bus."

These efforts only bring frustration initially, as she is not sure where Grissom stands with her, and clashes as well with his leadership of the team. This uncertainty is shown to not only affect them personally, but also starts to creep into their professional situation as well. Rumors abound in the department about a possible relationship between her and Grissom, and it's suggested that she is being passed up for a promotion because of it. In late season four, this frustration boils over in increasing drinking and run-ins with the others at work. She is suspended from work, and takes some time off to deal with her self-described "me problem" between 4.23 and 5.1. Eventually, she and Grissom do come together, after a troubled courtship over three seasons, and are reunited and married after his departure from the crime lab in 9.10.

As Grissom's criticism in 1.16 indicated, Sara has a tendency to become too emotionally involved in cases. Throughout her career, she gets distracted by particular cases, and loses track of her "proper" boundaries as a CSI. This happens most directly in cases involving sexual assault, as with the rape victim in 1.16 (and again with the same victim in 9.2, as she had been in a coma for eight years), the abused mail order brides in 5.13 (during which it is revealed that Sara herself grew up with an abusive, and ultimately murderous, mother), and the horrific multiple killings in 7.18. She also reacts badly to feeling manipulated, as in 4.4, 7.18, and at the hands of the conniving child prodigy Hannah West and her distraught brother, Marlon (in 6.18 and 8.7).

In the wake of her near-death experience in the desert in 8.1, after being kidnapped and left for dead by the Miniature Killer, Sara is shown to have a difficult time regaining enthusiasm for her job. Increasingly despondent, she tells Grissom in 8.5 that she's "sick of having death shoved in my face every day. The murder rate has gone up every year since I've been here. It's totally out of control, and we're not even slowing them down."[17] A series of devastating cases, including another encounter with the West siblings (resulting in Marlon's suicide and Hannah's subsequent emotional devastation), prompts her to resign CSI, suddenly leaving both Las Vegas and Grissom (whom she had agreed to marry earlier in season eight) in 8.7. In her goodbye letter to him (heard in voiceover as she takes a cab to the airport), she professes her love for him, but claims she "has to go." He ultimately comes to her, at her new research job in Costa Rica, in 9.10.

Eventually, however, despite her seemingly final decision to leave crime investigation, and her life with Grissom (now in Paris), she returns, in season 10, ostensibly to help the short-staffed team. In actuality, Sara is brought back due largely to the alleged failure of Jorja Fox's replacement, Lauren Lee Smith (as Riley Adams), to catch on with viewers, and the producers' desire to restore familiarity after William Petersen's departure. Showing more maturity and certainty, and now relishing her long relationships with Catherine, Nick, and Greg, Sara now seems to have accepted her particular professional and personal balance.

Warrick Brown (Gary Dourdan)

A soft-spoken, yet physically imposing figure, Warrick is regarded by his peers (including Grissom, on a few occasions) as the most thorough and effective criminalist of his rank. He is painstakingly meticulous in

Focus: Warrick tests a ladder for blood traces, in 7.5 "Double Cross."

the field, and quick to insure that the others are maintaining proper procedures as well (as shown most clearly in his criticism of Greg's sloppy field kit in 4.15). Grissom regards him as a natural leader, "the rock of my team," and occasionally gives him additional levels of responsibility, as in 2.10, when he leaves Warrick in charge of the team while he is out of town for a few days.[18] However, the tragic irony of Warrick's life is that, as stoic and methodical as he generally is at work (with some notable, and ultimately fatal, exceptions), he also sometimes loses control in his personal life. His gambling addiction is presented as a persistent source of doubt in the first two seasons, particularly since it indirectly causes the murder of rookie CSI Holly Gribbs in 1.1. Later, the stresses of his rash marriage in season six drive him to jealousy and pills, and ultimately to the reckless on-the-job behavior that lead to his brief suspension, and subsequent murder at the hands of the corrupt undersheriff McKeen (8.9, 8.10, 8.17).

As the only non-white member of the regular team, Warrick also carries a particular burden as a television character.[19] However, in the idealized world of the series (and in keeping with the representational codes of normative multi-cultural television drama of the 2000s), his race is only rarely made an issue. He sometimes deals more closely than the others with cases involving Black victims or suspects, as with the grandfather and grandson in 1.3 and 1.22, his former neighborhood mentor in 3.13, and the racist prison guards in 5.10. Significantly, Gary Dourdan's performance as Warrick is more stereotypically "black" in the first few episodes, and is then toned down considerably to the low-key, serious criminalist in the remainder of the run. While this is also something of a stereotype (at worst, the "noble minority"), Dourdan was able to keep Warrick credible, even while the writers did not always give him significant material to work with as consistently as they did with the other characters. Warrick, and race in general on *CSI*, is thus structured predominantly in what cultural historian Herman Gray calls an "assimilationist" discourse: he is physically and culturally African American, but functions only as an individual, rather than as a member of an historically-situated social group. Racism, when it is encountered on *CSI*, is generally rendered as an individual attitude rather than a structural problem. As Gray describes, "in these televisual worlds, American racial progress is measured by the extent to which individual citizens, regardless of color, class, or gender, are the same and are treated equally within the existing social, economic, and cultural (and televisual) order" (2004: 86).

Despite his considerable skills and outward calm, Warrick's fatal flaw (literally, in his case) is shown to be his inability to effectively balance his work demands and private life. His gambling haunts him in the first two seasons, and his hasty off-screen marriage to the previously unseen Tina (between 5.25 and 6.1) ends in divorce by season eight (though he had also fathered a child with her by then). Mostly, however, his frustrations with difficult problems or political barriers would boil over into anger and recklessness. This is particularly the case late in season eight, when his investigation into a shady strip club owner (Lou Gedda) leads him to have sex with a witness to one of Gedda's murders, who then ends up dead. When Warrick pushes the investigation, he discovers that corruption from inside the police has been hampering his investigation, and is framed for Gedda's murder. Undersheriff McKeen turns out to have been the source of corruption (unknown to Warrick), and he kills Warrick in 8.17, rather than risk being discovered.

In his eulogy in 9.1, before breaking up, Grissom praises Warrick for "his tenaciousness, his deep sense of loyalty, [and] his courage to risk his life for what he knew was right."[20] Atoning, finally, for his negligence in the death of Holly Gribbs years earlier, Warrick sacrifices himself to his principles. His adult life was bracketed by personal demons and professional limits, but in the end, Warrick surpasses both to do "what he knew was right."

Nick Stokes (George Eads)

The favorite son of a well-off Texas family, Nick is in most regards a conventional "action hero": youngish, attractive, and physically fit, he seems to conform to the usual TV stereotypes of the white male cop. However, Nick, particularly in the first few seasons of the series, while generally portrayed as steady and competent, is also shown to be a bit overreaching and thus insecure. He does not have the seemingly innate investigative skills that his peers Sara and Warrick do, and he knows it; he has to work harder at it. He tries to impress Grissom and take initiative, but sometimes fails at both. However, despite these issues, Grissom regards him as his best student. More than any of the others, Nick is quick to acknowledge his mistakes and seek to make amends. Despite the arguably greater technical skills displayed by others, he seems most comfortable in his role as criminalist. By season nine, with the departures of Sara, Warrick, and Grissom, his ascendancy to leadership is realized; he rises to second-in-command (under Catherine), and even inherits Grissom's office (though, in a typically generous move, he chooses to share it with the other CSIs).

While Sara is faulted for radiating suspicion and anger towards suspects, Nick is often criticized for the opposite problem. His greatest weakness is his too-ready empathy, on display on several occasions. His ill-conceived relationship with Christy Hopkins – a troubled prostitute who was found dead in 1.13, after he'd spent the night with her – almost destroyed his career early on. However this empathy also allows him to make important connections that others might miss. He often functions as a "good cop" in questioning, and uses his good-ol'-boy Texas demeanor to calm and disarm difficult people, as when he gently gets a teen boy to

Empathy: Nick calmly gets a teen boy to confess to masturbation, in order to account for traces of semen found on a shirt in the suspect's house, in 2.15 "Burden of Proof."

confess to masturbation in 2.15 when the team needed to account for semen on a piece of cloth in a bathroom. In 4.11, he goes out on a limb to reopen a missing persons case he feels is a homicide, despite Grissom's doubts, angrily defending his empathy: "That's who I am. That's how I do my job."[21] In 6.5, a hippie psychic even picks up on Nick's empathy, telling him he's "radiating this crazy feminine energy."[22]

His perceived weakness also places him in two highly dangerous situations, both beyond his control. In 2.19, he is stalked and terrorized by a crazed, voyeuristic loner (Crane) who has started spying on Nick and intercepting his e-mail. Seeing a profile of Nick in a LVPD newsletter, Crane decides to harass, threaten, and eventually attempt to kill Nick in his own apartment. Rather than save the day on his own, Nick is completely at Crane's mercy until Brass and the police arrive at the last minute to save him. Similarly, in the two-part fifth season finale (5.24–25), directed by cult film auteur Quentin Tarantino, Nick finds himself randomly kidnapped and buried underground in a glass coffin, kept alive with an air source by his captor only so the rest of the team could watch his torment via webcam. After nearly two days of the ordeal, Nick is only saved after

Grissom, watching online, successfully identifies the specific species of ant crawling on Nick's skin, and determines his location. Far from being conventionally heroic in this episode, Nick could not save himself, and nearly commits suicide (as his kidnapper had hoped). In the sixth season, Nick is still experiencing post-traumatic stress from this incident, and is uncomfortable around insects and small spaces. He is represented as unable to shake these feelings, and shown to be increasingly erratic, until his confidence is restored in 6.5, when he saves a doomed girl, the only survivor of a brutal family slaying.

However, his empathy is also his greatest asset in dealing with his colleagues. A few small feuds notwithstanding, Nick is arguably the most reliable "friend" any of the team has. He is particularly close with Warrick, with whom he shares off time and the occasional bet on the outcome of a case (or, in 5.1, whether or not the new DNA analyst would quit after one day), and intervenes when it becomes clear Warrick is abusing drugs in season eight. With Sara and Greg he is represented as more of a sibling: a protective (if sometimes jealous) brother with the former, and a teasing big brother with the latter.

Thus, while his openness and trust often leads him into trouble (e.g., in 4.1, when he accidentally let slip some information about a murder investigation to an old friend, who reports it to the media), it also helps him further his investigations (e.g., in 5.12, when his comfort around Mexican culture helps open doors in the narcocorrido murder). More than any other character, his professional abilities are humanized in this way.

Greg Sanders (Eric Szmanda)

During the first season of *CSI*, Greg is located exclusively in the lab, functioning as a geeky, highly intelligent, yet eager analyst. By the second season, he is anxious to move out in the field, and in 2.18 he finally gets his chance, assisting at a deadly bus accident in the desert. Although he is overwhelmed by the carnage at that scene, Sara, Nick, and Grissom reassure him that his help is valuable. Over the next few

FINDING BALANCE 77

Exuberance: Greg triumphantly shows off an incriminating evidence sample, in 2.16 "Primum Non Nocere."

years, Greg serves as both a rookie CSI and a lab tech (as the department was undermanned during that time). Since that time, Greg has been treated as an equal to Nick, Sara, and Warrick, and has even served as lead *CSI* in more recent cases.

Of all the team, Greg has thus had the most apparent path to adulthood. Indeed, unlike the other major characters, who were each coded as being around thirty at the time the series started, Greg was clearly in his mid-twenties: prone to immature jokes and awkward flirtations, and anxious to prove himself. Despite his eccentricities, the team recognizes his considerable skill and instincts in the lab early on. His initiative to look further back in the history of the two women involved in the murder of the businessman in 2.11 leads to their arrest. By the middle of season three, he's ready to officially make the move to the "field," and announces his intention to become a fully-fledged CSI. However, due to ongoing budget issues at the lab, he must continue his work there while he's training to become a criminalist, and is torn between these roles in seasons four and five. He proves his tenacity over this time, however. While he complains about his workload, he nevertheless performs his tasks with enormous skill and precision. He even accepts his deficiencies as a rookie CSI, accepting the "scut work" assigned him in his early cases, and failing at his first attempt at a proficiency exam in 5.1. In 5.11, he finally passes his proficiency, and becomes a CSI-1.

Along the way, however, despite his desire to become a CSI, the reality of their profession seems to affect Greg more than it does the others. That is, the labor of finding professional balance is most visible in Greg's actions and behaviors. He nearly passes out at the sight of the carnage at the bus accident in his first venture to the field in 2.18, and has a hard time dealing with the many grim rites of passage in his chosen work, including his first autopsy (5.2), his first burn victim (5.18), and his first dead child (5.10). He also physically takes on the dangers of CSI work. He is severely injured in the lab explosion indirectly caused by Catherine's negligence in 3.22. More significantly, he is almost killed by a violent gang following the accidental killing of Demetrius James in 7.4, and is nearly isolated by the department's official legal defense as they move to contain the potential political fallout in the subsequent coroner's inquest in 7.7. The physical and emotional repercussions from these events (particularly the beating in season seven) shake Greg. In later seasons, he is shown to be quieter, less effusive, and more serious. He has matured as a professional, but he's also been scarred by that passage.

Behind the Badges

CSI balances serial and episodic demands effectively and somewhat uniquely among its contemporaries. While not serialized nearly enough for many viewers, especially relative to most of the critical favorites of this century's television thus far (*The Sopranos, Lost, Mad Men*, etc.), the show's long-term success is still premised on our attraction and interest in its characters. Promo spots and hype about upcoming episodes are centered as much around these ongoing situations as they are the cases of the week.

Moreover, these tantalizing bits and pieces of personal lives have allowed a flowering of fan creativity, in the forms of fan fiction, fan art, and fan videos. While it is difficult to gauge the scope of *CSI*'s fan activities relative to other series, the show has inspired tens of thousands of stories posted online at various sites, including CSI-Forensics.com, Fanfiction.net, and many LiveJournal-based online communities. Stories, art, and "vids" (fan-produced video mashups of moments in the series, usually set to particular songs, a la music videos) generally focus on "shipping," that is, on the characters' emotional, romantic and/or sexual relationships with each other, rather than offer new cases for them to solve. *CSI*'s relative paucity of definitive on-screen moments in these relationships leaves a wide-open terrain for fan speculation and desire, which these works enthusiastically fill in. Importantly, fans have produced works that not only cover the series' "official" established relationships (e.g., Grissom/Sara, Grissom/Lady Heather, Hodges/Wendy), but plausibly expand into other couplings, whether hetero (Sara/Nick, Catherine/Warrick), homo (Nick/Greg, Catherine/Sara), or beyond (Catherine/Nick/Greg). While certainly not acknowledged as canonical by the producers, these works are important fora for fan expression, deepening ongoing interest in the series, and extending its characters' virtual lives in innovative and entertaining ways.

These stories, vids, and other works are perhaps the ultimate vindication of the series' subtle serial narrative. Fans are engaged with the characters' ongoing stories as much if not more than the "case of the week" mysteries. In addition, as this overview has shown, *CSI*'s particular approach to seriality arguably says more about modern adulthood (or more specifically, about the normative media representations of modern adulthood) than the more volatile narratives a typical serial might plausibly convey. Most people show up to work and do their jobs day in and day out. Change is largely incremental, like Greg's becoming a CSI, or Grissom opening his heart to Sara, taking place over months and years, with confusion and setbacks along the way. Change can also be sudden, like losing one's father, or one's life, with repercussions that resonate long after the event. *CSI*'s narrative structure acknowledges change at both these registers, and allows its characters the room to deal with it, yet still go on with their lives.

Beyond commanding viewers and inspiring fans however, *CSI* has also allegedly had a considerable impact on popular culture more broadly during its run. The various "effects" attributed to it will be examined in the closing chapter.

Chapter 4
CSI Effects

> *There's too many forensic shows on TV.*
> (Grissom, 6.17, "I Like To Watch")[1]

What is the power of popular television? As we have seen, *CSI* certainly works as a contemporary crime drama through its singular narrative and audiovisual style, complex use of setting, and subtle serial storytelling. However, these factors still do not explain its long-term popularity nor, more importantly, the myriad cultural, industrial, and even legal effects that have been attributed to it over its run. Given the television industry's spotty track record in predicting hits, it is difficult enough to understand what attracts viewers to a program before the question of broader effects can even be raised. Nevertheless, television obviously matters, and matters in many ways, otherwise books like these would never be published or read, industries would not depend on it to prosper, and billions of us would not watch or discuss it. This chapter takes on this fundamental issue – does *CSI* matter? – by considering the thorny issue of what the series has done to the world beyond the boundaries of its episodes. While this is hardly the standard way to frame such a question in humanities-based cultural criticism (where "effects" are generally eschewed in favor of more ambiguous, and ambivalent, terms like "discourse"), the treatment of *CSI* in the public sphere has begged the question. There are, allegedly, "*CSI* Effects," which (again, allegedly) have impacted the functioning of criminal justice systems, the design of and enrollment in degree programs in forensic science, and the cultural appetite for crime fiction and non-fiction on television and across all media. In order to understand these "effects," we must not accept their claims at face value, but trace how they came to be attributed to *CSI* in the first place. Any reference to a "*CSI* Effect" is itself a media production, generated by a complex array of cultural forces, including academia, journalism, governments, media industry hype, and even the program itself.

The question of media effects is situated within long, complex debates in media studies. While the contentious history of this issue is much too extensive to explore here, suffice it to say that while the critical consensus (of both cultural studies/humanities-based researchers and social scientists) is that media influences society (and, in principle, vice versa), there is substantial disagreement regarding the nature and extent of that influence, and how it could, or even should be, measured. For the purposes of this chapter, I regard the issue of effects as an already-mediated concept. That is, we cannot approach the question of influence/effects/significance/discourse without acknowledging the contexts in which such a claim is circulated. In this case, *CSI*'s key "effect" is undeniably its broad function as popular – and to a significant extent, popu*list* – branded entertainment: it generates normative expectations of drama, spectacle, science, criminal investigation, and commercial media to a large audience. Each of these categories is packaged and cited in every iteration of *CSI*, from the original series, through its spinoffs, ancillary media, licensed merchandise, associated media texts, citations in journalism and throughout popular media, assessments in industry trade media, and even mentions in court proceedings.

Along the way, three interrelated, though ultimately discontinuous realms converge upon representations of forensic science in general, and *CSI* specifically: legal culture, scientific culture, and popular culture. Each of these areas seemingly operates with its own conventions, rituals, and logics. However, each must also draw upon the others when connecting with broader concerns. Forensic science has been the nexus of these areas since at least the 1990s. Developments in laboratory science (e.g., DNA analysis) are described and narrativized in journalistic, documentary, and dramatic accounts, and debated and incorporated into legal policies, if not outright legislation. Even as a broad, often poorly understood concept, forensic science has important implications in each of these discursive forms, prompting new practices and technologies of detection, generating intrigue and excitement in media accounts, and ultimately affecting how our society functions in the areas of medicine and criminal justice. These areas may function independently, but they ultimately rely on each other for social engagement. As Gray Cavender and Sarah K. Deutsch argue, *CSI* conspicuously brings these concerns together. "Science stands for truth on *CSI*, truth in a deeper philosophical sense, and in terms of the case at hand, that is, proving who is the criminal. But, because this is television, science must also be entertaining and accessible" (2007: 74). Moreover, the pedagogical address of the series (as analyzed in chapter 1) is seen to legitimate its treatment of science, particularly for its producers, as when Associate Producer Naren Shankar defends *CSI*'s educational value in a magazine interview: "[Nowadays] you don't have to tell a jury what DNA can do and these other things that used to require days of testimony. People understand the evidentiary value of forensics, and that's connected to the show."[2]

This chapter explores how *CSI*, and more broadly, discourses of "*CSI* Effects," have combined these areas, blurring the ostensible boundaries between spectacle and science, and challenging efforts (from the courts in particular) to keep entertainment and information separate. The effects attributed to *CSI* actually begin with its inception as a CBS television program, and its subsequent expansion into spinoffs, related programs, and other media. They escalate with descriptions of *CSI* Effects in courtrooms across the US, and in the scholarly analyses that followed. Finally, I locate them back where they ostensibly originate: in *CSI* itself, where the text has offered its own mediation of its ostensible effects, and the relationships between legal, scientific, and popular cultures.

The *CSI* Franchise

The primary, indisputable "effect" that can be traced to *CSI* is what it has done for its producers, stars, network, genre, and even television as a medium. Simply put, the series has been a phenomenal financial and popular success, almost from the moment of its debut in the fall of 2000. As noted in chapter 1, it has consistently scored near the top of the year-end Nielsen television ratings (only regularly displaced till recently by reality juggernauts *American Idol* and *Dancing With The Stars*), and as of the end of its ninth season (2008–9) was still the top-ranked scripted series on American television. Its spinoffs, *CSI: Miami* (2002–) and *CSI: NY* (2004–) also consistently rank in the Nielsen top 20. Moreover, each series has in turn sold well to other countries, making *CSI* a global brand.[3] More extensively and impressively, its many spin-offs have also gained similar stature, making forensic-driven crime dramas the most watched scripted genre on all of American television, and forensic-based reality series a staple on many cable channels. This success on television, both for *CSI* and the many programs in its cultural and industrial wake, has spilled over into other media forms, including non-fiction books, prose and graphic novels, video games, and museum exhibits. By the end of its first decade, *CSI* had clearly become one of television's all-time greatest popular successes, generating a sustainable entertainment franchise, and inspiring a stable of similar properties.

While it is tempting in retrospect to view *CSI* as "lighting in a bottle," that is, a once-in-a-generation combination of ideas, people, and timing, the broad context of crime and justice-themed entertainment and infotainment at the time of its inception should be considered. Interest in mediated forensic science had already begun to expand before *CSI* premiered. The Menendez and Simpson murder trials were long-running media spectacles in the 1990s, televised virtually gavel-to-gavel by Court TV, and covered extensively by CNN and broadcast news outlets. Details of these crimes, including forensic evidence, became part of the standard media diet at that time. Elayne Rapping has argued that these trials, and the news, documentary, and reality programming that ballooned across cable and broadcast television at this time, presented a vital window into critical areas of American social, cultural, and political life. They rendered the criminal justice system into a compelling audiovisual melodrama that still commands much attention (2003: 103–37). In the wake of these trials, which consistently drew millions of viewers and steady publicity, several documentary series and non-fiction books were released that focused on forensic science and crime investigation. Long-running reality television series like *American Justice* (1992–), *Cold Case Files* (1999–), *Forensic Files* (originally *Medical Detectives*, 1996–), *The New Detectives* (1996–2004, and reportedly the direct inspiration for *CSI*), and others became staples of cable and satellite channels like A&E, Discovery, and Court TV (now TruTV), offering "real-life" examples of crime scene investigation, typically observing actual criminalists performing the same tasks seen later on *CSI*: gathering evidence, processing materials in the lab, and performing autopsies. These series also typically mix actuality with reenactment, as interviews are often mixed with an observational documentary style and dramatized versions of the events described. In addition, these series are presented with a familiar spectacular sheen, utilizing pictorial digital effects (e.g., on-screen graphics and animations) and expressionistic editing to enhance the "real" drama. Thus, although its specific roots lie in creator Anthony Zuiker's research and experiences with Las Vegas criminalists, it is important to remember that *CSI* was pitched to the networks in this environment, where spectacular forensic-based investigation series were already an increasingly prevalent reality subgenre, but had not yet inspired any scripted dramas.

It is important to remember as well what was happening at CBS at this time. During the second half of the 1990s, the network had struggled in the ratings, regularly falling behind not only to the then-perpetual leader NBC, but also to the other two major broadcast networks, ABC and Fox. As Victoria Johnson notes, CBS' 1990s schedule of safe, middlebrow fare like *Dr. Quinn, Medicine Woman* (1993–8), *Promised Land* (1996–9), and *Touched By An Angel* (1994–2003) had cemented its status as a conservative, "heartland"-centric network, at the expense of critical acclaim, popular buzz, and enough of the critical 18–49 year-old demographic favored by advertisers (2008: 202–6). Even its crime dramas, which included *Diagnosis Murder* (1992–2001), *Nash Bridges* (1996–2001), *Walker, Texas Ranger* (1993–2001), and the long-running *Murder, She Wrote* (1984–96), seemed like staid, formulaic 1970s relics, out of synch in an era of envelope-pushing fare like *NYPD Blue* (ABC, 1993–2004), *The X-Files* (Fox, 1993–2002), and *Homicide: Life on the Streets* (NBC, 1993–9).

In 2000, CBS made the critical decision to debut two series that would adjust this image: *CSI* and *Survivor*. The latter, itself the legitimate subject of extended scholarly analysis, was an instant and unforeseen sensation during its initial summer 2000 run, and has reasonably been credited with validating reality television (and particularly the reality competition format) as viable network prime-time programming. *CSI* was famously the last series added to CBS' 2000–1 schedule. Its success was not guaranteed; its development seemingly made it a long shot to even reach the CBS prime-time schedule, let alone achieve massive popularity. Neither creator Zuiker nor producer Jerry Bruckheimer had achieved any success on television. The other three major networks all passed on the *CSI* script. CBS, intrigued mostly by Bruckheimer's desire to bring his signature feature-film panache – as seen most prominently in brash and loud action films like *Top Gun* (1986), *The Rock* (1996), *Con Air* (1997), and *Armageddon* (1998) – to the small screen, commissioned a pilot and then a series. While the final financing almost fell through (Canadian media company Alliance Atlantis replacing Disney subsidiary Touchstone Television at the eleventh hour), the series went into production and was put on the schedule. It debuted on Friday, October 6, 2000 and was an immediate hit, outranking its higher-profiled lead-in, a remake of the 1960s series *The Fugitive*, right out of the gate.[4] Its virtually instant success vaulted its cast and crew – most of whom were relatively unknown previously – into the top tier of the television industry.[5] In early 2001, CBS moved *CSI*, along with the second season of *Survivor*, to Thursdays, to take advantage of the perceived vulnerability of NBC's aging "must-see" lineup, which had started to slip after the end of *Seinfeld* in 1998. By 2002, on the strength of *Survivor* and *CSI*, CBS came to dominate the night.[6]

That was only the beginning, however. *CSI*'s surprise success revealed a surprisingly unmet viewer appetite for cutting-edge crime drama, despite the prevalence of the genre on network schedules for years. As NBC had already spun off its steadily growing *Law & Order* in 1999 (with *Law & Order: Special Victims Unit*), CBS immediately began developing a *CSI* spinoff. Since CBS considered the series' focus on forensic science and its use of its Las Vegas setting as its most striking features, it decided to maintain the focus on science and spectacle but exploit other similarly intriguing locales. Introduced to viewers with a "backdoor pilot" crossover episode of *CSI* ("Cross Jurisdictions," episode 2.22) in May 2002, *CSI: Miami* debuted on September 2002 and was an immediate success in its late Monday time slot. Though not as critically well regarded as the original, the series successfully transplanted the *CSI* formula to a new, even more picturesque setting, which fostered different crime plots and characters, as well as "beach appeal," which provided new frontiers of spectacle.[7] A second spinoff, *CSI: NY*, debuted in September 2004, bringing a wintry, slightly grimmer, post-9/11 sensibility to what had been exclusively a sun belt franchise. Although each series adheres closely to the standard *CSI* formula as described in previous chapters (including theme songs by the Who: "Who Are You," for *CSI*, "Won't Get Fooled Again" for *CSI: Miami* and "Baba O'Riley" for *CSI: NY*), differences in characters and setting have enabled some slight variations, particularly in terms of cinematography and production design, in order to distinguish each.

While the three *CSI* series were integral to CBS' success in the 2000s, this particular "*CSI* Effect" has been even more extensive on the network. Several additional, similarly-themed series (many of which also produced by Jerry Bruckheimer) debuted in the wake of *CSI's* success, to the point that the "C" in CBS might as well have stood for "crime." In the 2008–9 season, CBS had no less than 11 regularly scheduled crime dramas on the air, half of its total prime-time schedule. Each of them centered on a team of investigators solving difficult crimes in stylized, spectacular narratives, though each also had a particular twist. *NCIS* (2003–) (which debuted its own spinoff, *NCIS: Los Angeles*, in September 2009) is concerned with crimes involving military personnel. *Cold Case* (2003–10), heavily utilizing flashbacks and period detail, investigates long-dormant crimes. Following Gil Grissom's lead, *Criminal Minds* (2005–), *Numb3rs* (2005–10), *The Mentalist* (2008–), and *Without A Trace* (2002–9) all tout intriguing and slightly eccentric lead characters with particularly attuned analytical skills. Cementing these similarities further, a few of these series have aired crossover episodes alongside characters from neighboring crime shows, thus transforming much of CBS' schedule into a coherent "universe" of characters and settings, all emanating from the original *CSI*.[8]

While this television dominance has been *CSI*'s primary industrial effect, it has also been successfully expanded to other forms, widening its footprint across several media platforms. Like other successful multi-media properties (e.g., Harry Potter, *Star Trek*, *Star Wars*), *CSI* quickly became a distinctive brand that delivers similar experiences despite different media forms. Lines of licensed original prose and graphic novels (from Pocket Books and IDW Publishing, respectively) based on each incarnation of the franchise have extended *CSI* onto the printed page, with narratives that successfully emulate the style of the television episodes. Similarly, several non-fiction books, including the lushly illustrated coffee table volume, *Ultimate CSI*, offer not only guides to the series' production, but also extended definitions and details about the characters' procedures and tools, further extending the pedagogical remit of the series.

The *CSI* video games, published by Ubisoft primarily for the PC platform, are particularly exemplary in this regard, and worth considering here in some detail. Each of the six games released so far (four based on the original *CSI*, and one each based on *CSI: Miami* and *CSI: NY*) places the player directly in the forensics team as a novice criminalist. Using a mouse and keyboard, a player must learn and successfully perform the skills typically shown in the series, such as identifying potential evidence on the scene, dusting for fingerprints, processing evidence in the lab, and questioning suspects. Each game has featured the voice performances and digital likenesses of most of the main cast from the television series. However, the games have also been criticized for hewing too closely and predictably to the series' standard episodic formula. In his review of the fourth *CSI* title, *CSI: Hard Evidence*, Gamespot's Alex Navarro complained that the *CSI* games "are less games and more mediocre episodes of the TV show that require button presses to unfold."[9] Each release consists of several individual criminal cases of gradually ascending difficulty, which must be solved consecutively to complete the game. Tasks are generally laid out in a single sequence, with each step only advancing when it has been correctly completed. As the games' critics have noted, this removes most of the suspense and detective work from the narrative, as players can only progress based on their dexterity within a very circumscribed set of skills. Moreover, as Navarro argued, the typical game narrative follows a relatively caricatured version of a typical *CSI* plot. For example, the third suspect questioned in most interrogation scenes is almost always revealed to be the killer.

As a virtual member of the team, the player is treated as a rookie criminalist. Established characters function as instructors, lecturing players about proper procedures, and chiding them for their mistakes. While players have to heed that advice and follow explicit directions in order to move forward, they don't have any opportunities for further interactions that could take the game in different directions. A player cannot flirt with Catherine or Warrick, for example, or find additional evidence, or even collaborate with other human players, as the game is only available as an offline, single-player, self-contained experience. Similar limitations on content and the range of interactivity notoriously plague most licensed game adaptations of properties that originate in other media forms (e.g., games based on film, TV, or comic book characters), but they are particularly acute in the *CSI* games. While they are as functionally "educational," in an informative sense at least, as the series itself, they feel more like exams testing the player's knowledge of *CSI*'s forensic practices than an immersive interactive world. That said, they have still adequately fulfilled their primary role as *CSI*-branded entertainment products, and have sold well enough in the market thus far to come out almost annually.

The *CSI* franchise has even extended into real space, by way of a travelling exhibit at science museums, and a permanent attraction at the MGM Grand hotel in Las Vegas, which opened in the summer of 2009. In each of these explicitly pedagogical incarnations, the *CSI* brand functions as the imprimatur of a particular understanding of forensic science. Indeed, the very concept "forensic science" is identified squarely with the *CSI* brand in these exhibits. In the travelling *CSI: The Experience*, museum patrons are drafted as criminalists (by way of reality-bending interactive videos featuring in-character cast members and real criminalists), and presented with a variety of forensic evidence corresponding to three different crime scenes (each similar to typical cases found on the original series). They are instructed on how to gather and analyze evidence, and asked to present their findings at the end of the exhibit (appropriately, a replica of Gil Grissom's office). The mission statement of the exhibit is to "invite people to use real science to solve hypothetical crimes in an exciting multimedia environment."[10] While this description refers directly to *CSI: The Experience*, its melding of science, spectacle, and entertainment could also apply to the entire franchise.

Forensic Science as Popular Culture

As the science-as-spectacle aesthetic and ethos of *CSI* has dominated prime-time television, and spread to other media, it has arguably bled over from *popular* to *public culture*: regarded not only as entertainment, but also as a means by which to understand and function in the world more broadly. This is where the issue of its ostensible "effects" begins to become contentious, as it often does in regard to entertainment television in general. The key question: has *CSI* literally changed the way citizens understand crimes, investigation, and the entire justice system?

As the last 15 years have indicated, such enhanced, yet routine media exposure of crime and justice, of which *CSI* is only the most prominent component, presents particular visions of the American criminal justice system. Centrally, this programming offers a justice system that functions as a stage for moral drama, where "good guys" and "bad guys" battle, using the tools of language and technology to make their cases. While it seems inevitable that such accounts would affect participants in the actual justice system, from judges to jurors and everyone in between, the question of effect is not so easily answered, nor indeed, even easily questioned. How can one begin to approach it, and separate the impact of fictional television programming from other influences?

Direct observation is a useful place to start. Jury duty, for example, is one of the few common civic experiences most adult Americans encounter over their lives. While it is still a task with direct bearing on the functioning of society, it is striking how judges, prosecutors, defense attorneys, and even the instructional videos shown in waiting rooms routinely compare this ostensibly portentous act of citizenship to its film and TV representations.[11] As Rapping points out, courtrooms are places viewed most of the time as entertainment much more than experienced as important work; they seem more cultural than social. In these spaces, after all, are conflict, melodrama, power, intrigue, and ritual: all things typically found in an episode of *CSI* or any other crime or courtroom drama. Accordingly, even in its own spaces, the legal system has had a difficult time coping with the differences between the legal reality of criminal justice proceedings and the cultural unreality of crime fiction. This has particularly, and infamously, been the situation over the past decade, as *CSI*, its spinoffs, and many other similarly-themed television series have dramatized forensic science, and have allegedly fostered problematic jury expectations about the function of evidence in criminal trials. However, many years after this so-called "*CSI* Effect" was first referenced, the real effect seems to have been more on how the principles and practices of forensic science are handled by prosecutors, defense attorneys, court officials, and media coverage, rather than any demonstrable impact of the series itself on jury behavior. As Simon A. Cole and Rachel Dioso-Villa put it in their important 2007 overview of the *CSI* Effect, it would be more appropriate to deem it the relevant factor the "*CSI* Effect *Effect*": "the effect of media about the *CSI* Effect on criminal trials" (2007: 468).

According to Cole and Dioso-Villa, the "*CSI* Effect" was first described in 2002 in press reports of prosecutors complaining that jurors were starting to have "unrealistic" standards for forensic evidence, ostensibly based on what they had seen in *CSI* and similar series (2007: 445–6). While, as we've seen, the evidence is sacrosanct on *CSI*, and nearly always produces the emphatic, capital-T "Truth" about a suspect's guilt, real evidence standards are much less definitive. As Cole and Dioso-Villa argue, the American legal standard of "beyond a reasonable doubt" is much more ambiguous than the seeming scientific certainty that *CSI* is premised on (2007: 465–8). This standard does not eradicate all doubt, but places a contingent limit (i.e., the "reasonable") upon it. Moreover, even science itself doesn't rely upon the absolute standards of proof typically seen on *CSI*. According to New York City criminalist Lisa Faber, actual evidence in a criminal investigation is never described as an absolute "match," but rather with terms like "could have come from" or "is associated with," which suggest correlation and likeness, but are not presented as "open and shut" markers of individual identity (Quoted in Toobin, 2007: 33). Similarly, evidence that is often presented in *CSI* as conclusive, like ear prints, bite marks, and handwriting, is often inadmissible in reality. In addition, *CSI*'s seemingly infallible computer analyses have obscured the reality that human forensic scientists, not machines, still ultimately evaluate the evidence. As Michael Mopas points out, justice on *CSI* is not presented as "a social endeavour that is open to the possibility of human error, but something that can be done quickly, automatically and accurately within the laboratory" (2007: 111). This is particularly the case with DNA analysis. While it is presented as the go-to standard on the series, and has shown significant promise as a tool thus far in reality, DNA analysis is more costly, time-consuming, and ambiguous in actual criminal investigation and legal practice than it is in Grissom's crime lab. As journalist Kit Roane reported in his 2005 analysis of the *CSI* Effect, "everyone, including the jury, wants certainty. But it seldom exists in forensics." (2005: 54). Thus, many prosecutors have argued that, even in cases which would have most likely resulted in convictions under prevailing norms of proof, jurors have been dubious enough, due to the lack of rock-solid certainty about the physical evidence that the TV series' criminalists and practices project in their cases, that they would vote to acquit.

While this would be a worrying trend, the problem, as several legal scholars, psychologists, and sociologists have researched, is that it has yet to be verified. To date, there have been only a handful of studies that have tested whether or not the *CSI* Effect on juries actually exists. The consensus thus far is, appropriately, inconclusive, suggesting that while jurors are becoming somewhat more critical of forensic evidence in trials, it is difficult to separate their viewing of *CSI* from anything else they may have encountered in popular culture. For example, assessing a jury in a mock trial they designed, N. J. Schweitzer and Michael J. Saks found in their 2007 study that while viewers of *CSI* and/or other forensic crime shows were more critical of forensic evidence in the trial, and slightly less likely to vote to convict, they did not feel that there was a substantial statistical difference between viewers and non-viewers. Similarly, as Cole and Dioso-Villa point out, data from Federal trials reveals that if anything, acquittals have actually decreased since *CSI*'s premiere in 2000 (2007: 461–2).

However, its effect on the attitudes of lawyers and judges, and the tenor of media coverage of the ostensible *CSI* Effect, has been much more apparent. Describing the *CSI* Effect as more of a "moral panic" than an actual issue, Cole and Dioso-Villa argue that its accumulated discursive weight in legal culture is the critical factor, citing it "as an example of the way that a broad consensus about the existence of a legally relevant 'fact' can emerge out of unsystematic and untested anecdotal observations" (2007: 464). They cite a study of the Maricopa County, Arizona court system that claimed to prove the existence of the effect on jurors, but actually measured *prosecutors*' beliefs that the effect already exists in most of their potential jurors. Moreover, despite prosecutors' complaints about *CSI*, all the discourse surrounding the ostensible *CSI* Effect has benefited them; as Cole and Dioso-Villa shrewdly suggest, "[they] have turned a television show that may well enhance the credibility of forensic evidence into a perceived liability, convinced the media that prosecutors are now unfairly disadvantaged in the typical US criminal trial, and turned the acquittals into an apparent social problem" (2007: 464).

Moreover, the ostensible effects described by media coverage are widespread. Cole and Dioso-Villa describe no fewer than six *CSI* Effects that have been attributed to the series, ranging from the alleged reduction in convictions to the spike in interest in forensic science majors at colleges and universities (2007: 447–52). Most tellingly, anxiety about the *CSI* Effect has effectively been used by justice systems and organizations at every level to lobby for greater funding for and education about forensic science, as the Crime Lab Project did when it drew from *CSI*'s popularity while rejecting its realist claims, and the National District Attorney Association did when it used George Eads (CSI's Nick Stokes) in its PSAs to support the public image of prosecutors.

Mediating the *CSI* Effect, in *CSI*

Despite the meticulously crafted drama and aesthetics that have driven *CSI* so successfully for a decade, the series' own publicity has generally emphasized its use of "real" and "accurate" forensic technologies and practices, attempting to stake at least a partial claim to truth. The tenor of much of this forensics-related publicity is proud, if somewhat defensive, asserting that they (the producers) really know what they are talking about, and if they do not, they ask someone who does. To that end, former criminalists Elizabeth Devine and Richard Catalani have prominently functioned as technical consultants, writers, and producers on all three *CSI* series at various times.[12] Accordingly, they have not only helped verify that the series is being reasonably accurate in its use of forensic practices (again, with a wide dramatic license); they also regularly help shape storylines. More importantly for the sake of publicity, they have also been featured in media interviews about *CSI* and forensic science more generally. On several of the *CSI* DVD box sets, they have offered tours of the *CSI* lab and demonstrations of its practices and technologies, emphasizing that these are (or are close to) the same tools used in the "real world." For example, on the second season set, Devine points out and describes various pieces of lab equipment, like dual comparison microscopes, or the GC/MS (Gas Chromatograph/Mass Spectrometer, used to identify the chemical composition of trace materials), intercut with clips of the items in use in the series.[13] Reality and fiction effectively collide in this feature, as Devine takes viewers through not a real crime lab, but the *CSI* set. The "reality" of the devices she describes is as much the verification of their use onscreen (in the brief clips of episodes) as it is her verification (as a real criminalist) of their use in actual investigations.

Similarly, an extra titled "The Research of *CSI*: Maintaining The Accuracy," on the season five set features interviews with several Las Vegas criminalists who had been consulted in the production of the series who all testify to the accuracy of the series, yet still allow that the formal requirements of television drama sometimes trump the desire for accuracy (e.g., most forensics lab tests take days or even weeks; on

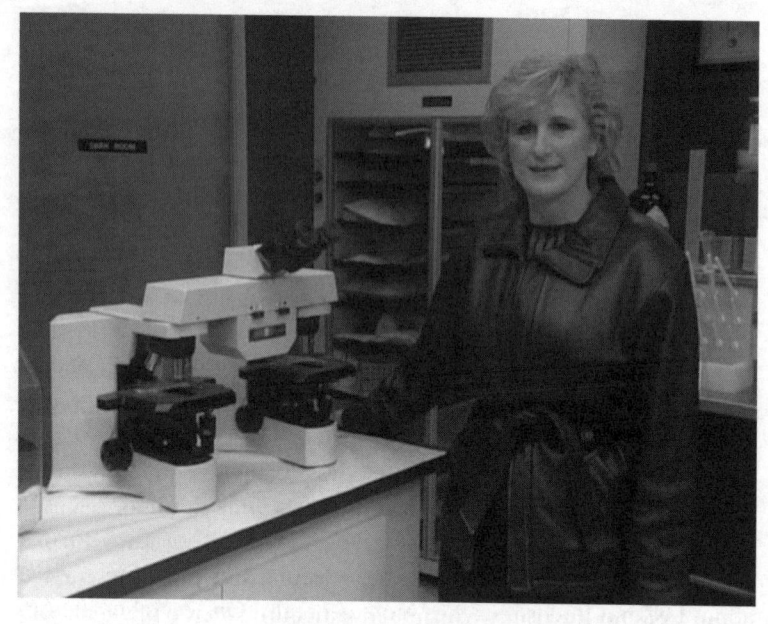

Reality/fiction: Technical consultant and former criminalist Elizabeth Devine displays real lab equipment on the CSI set, like this polarized light microscope, in a behind-the-scenes feature on the Season 2 box set.

CSI, they are typically done in minutes or hours). In the same piece, several writers (including showrunner Carol Mendelsohn) and staff researchers David Berman and Jon Wellner (who also play assistant coroner David Phillips and toxicologist Henry Andrews in the series) explain how they work with their regular advisors, and hundreds of other expert contacts, in order to keep the series as accurate as possible yet still tell compelling stories. In all of these "behind the scenes" materials, which also include publications like the 2006 book *Ultimate CSI*, which blends real descriptions of actual forensic tools and techniques with character biographies and case reports drawn from *CSI* episodes, drama is both compared to and distinguished from reality. Thus, the ingredients for the ostensible "*CSI* Effects" are not only built into the design of the show; they are one of the primary ways producers, distributors, and others have promoted the series.

The public debates about *CSI*'s entertainment and pedagogical functions have also played out in some episodes of the series, as the team grapples with media coverage and courtroom procedure. What's striking about these instances is how the various *CSI* Effects – concerns about how evidence is processed and used – are presented as burdensome obstacles to their more important work of finding the truth and "speaking for the dead," as Grissom has put it on occasion. The media in particular is almost always depicted in *CSI* as an annoyance at best, and dangerous at worst. Episode 6.17, appropriately titled "I Like to Watch," is a particularly intriguing example of this tendency. In the episode, the team are themselves the subject of a reality television program. Throughout the episode, they are followed by a reality TV camera crew, and questioned by an off-screen director. While the mediated construction of ostensible reality is explored in this episode, the "reality" that we compare it to is not "reality" *per se*, but rather the reality of *CSI* as we have come to know it (after six seasons, at that point in time). In other words, a more typical *CSI* episode is presented as our basis for the reality of crime investigation, on top of which 6.17 places a layer of reflexive mediation. For example, when the unseen reality show director presses Sofia on her "allegiance" to the cops or CSIs (she had been a CSI in season five, and was now a detective in season six), she angrily tells him that both are on the "same side" of the fence. Her denial of such conflict belies the fact that the series itself amplifies the cop-vs.-criminalist tension on a recurrent basis, not least in an extended arc earlier in the same season, in the aftermath of the events of 6.7 (when a car chase ends with a shootout between police and suspects, resulting in the accidental death of one officer from friendly fire from Brass' gun). In a similar, but much more intentional poke at their own mediation of forensics, Nick chides Hodges for trying to pose and look important for the camera during a six-hour lab process. Hodges retorts "when they cut it together, it'll only take thirty seconds."[14]

One of the key sources of drama on the series concerns the team's credibility as forensic scientists. The "classic" *CSI* Effect suggests that the series' depictions of forensic technologies and practices as infallible truth machines render real forensics systems inadequate. The treatment

Watching the detectives: Catherine and Grissom encounter a reality TV camera crew, in 6.17 "I Like To Watch."

of the CSIs on the series itself bears out this critique, as the LVPD's forensics unit's investigative standards are considered so high that they are rarely questioned. While defense attorneys and their clients may express incredulity at some evidence in the interrogation room, their doubts are usually dispatched as one of the criminalists calmly explains what the evidence means. At that point, the gig, as they say, is usually up. Moreover, the functioning of CSIs as de facto detectives, with direct contact with suspects and witnesses (something that would not only not occur in reality; it would usually be regarded as a serious ethical breach) raises their agency dramatically, placing them in the driver's seat of the whole investigation process. Any problems that do arise with the ways the criminalists gather or process evidence are generally presented as temporary individual mistakes usually caused by exhaustion or stress (as in Catherine's carelessness which results in the lab explosion in 3.22), or, more commonly, as systemic or political issues with *other* LVPD sections, past or present (e.g., the rarely-seen but seemingly inept "day shift" of the first few seasons, or the inadequate evidence standards of the past, as seen in 7.12).

Potential problems of this regard in the narrative are also immediately treated as problems of publicity, and therefore as political. The

Mediated justice: Brass, Grissom and Warrick meet the press after the arrest of Hollywood star Tom Havilland, in 3.2 "The Accused Is Entitled."

various supervisors, undersheriffs, sheriffs, and district attorneys depicted in the series generally only appear when the prospect of bad publicity looms, particularly in high-profile cases (e.g., the baby found in the hot car in 4.4, the murder of a prominent community activist in 7.13, the murder of a key witness in a grand jury case in 8.12). At these points, the team struggles to do its work ethically but also loyally, that is, keeping or restoring the image not only of the team, but of the department and thus of the State as a valid and effective government. However, the implication is consistently given that our CSIs are above politics, and that they ultimately care most about serving justice, and each other, rather than appeasing the "higher-ups," regardless of the circumstances. Accordingly, their occasional antagonism with department officials (and occasionally with detectives and uniformed cops, defense lawyers or the media) over their methods or findings ultimately functions to reassure us that they have the ethical higher ground: they are looking out for capital-J Justice, rather than protecting their jobs.

The most extended example of such tensions about control and credibility was the "team in jeopardy" arc that took up most of season five. Grissom's primary nemesis, day-shift supervisor Conrad Ecklie (played by Marc Vann), is promoted above him, and immediately starts criticizing Grissom's allegedly lax management of his team. While not portrayed as an outright villain, Ecklie is typically used in this story arc to personify naked political ambition, "reining in" the ostensible excesses of Grissom and his team to bolster his own career in the department. In 5.9, Ecklie splits up the team, and reassigns Catherine, Nick, and Warrick to a swing shift; they are only brought back together after Nick's harrowing ordeal in the glass coffin in 5.25. In between, each functions with a higher degree of discomfort and self-awareness than previously, knowing that Ecklie is closely scrutinizing their performance and behavior. Issues of leadership, politics, and professional ethics thread through the entire season, as individual, team, and department credibility are questioned. While this was an especially long arc for *CSI*, these issues have appeared throughout the series' run, and indeed in television police drama more broadly, as concerns about public appearance and loyalty are rendered against the protagonists' concerns for justice and each other. In 8.3, one of her last episodes (before her season 10 return), as Sara becomes progressively disenchanted with her work as a CSI, she investigates the wrongful death of a homeless man at the hands of negligent police officers. When rookie CSI Ronnie Lake expresses surprise that Sara is going to accuse the cops, Sara tells her that their commitment to the truth should come first, no matter the political circumstances: "We're not here to protect anyone, Ronnie, not even the cops. We're here to figure out what happened. If you can't do that, you should get a different job."[15]

This Grissom-esque mantra to "figure out what happened" is a virtual definition of both the series' avowed scientific ethos, and the heroic function of its principals. However, as the ultimate fate of Warrick (as described in the last chapter) makes clear, characters are often punished for going beyond "figuring out what happened" to "avenging what happened," or "attempting to prevent something happening." Their heroism is ostensibly one of reaffirming an ideal of impartial science, rather than intervening in a criminal or unjust act. Of course, in order to heighten the drama and bolster our sympathy for the characters, they occasionally move from investigation into more direct action. One of these decisions takes a particularly difficult turn for Greg in season seven.

In 7.4, Greg is nearly beaten to death in an alley by a vengeful mob of masked assailants after he intervenes in another man's beating by accidentally hitting and killing one of the gang members with his car. Three episodes later, and still traumatized by the incident, he has to take the stand in the coroner's inquest about the boy's (Demetrius James) death. Due of the nature of that particular legal proceeding, which allows direct questioning of witnesses from members of the jury, Greg must endure accusations of police brutality, racism, and even DWI (he had had one glass of wine hours before the incident). While these are all serious accusations, they are rendered highly dubious in this context because of our built-up affinity for Greg after many years. Since we know him, and we saw what happened in that alley, viewer sympathies are unquestionably with Greg. While the jury, the victim's family, and even the judge (who is apparently running for a higher office and courting potential constituents) seem set against Greg, Nick and Warrick walk through an intricate 3D computer reenactment of the incident, reassembled from the data of eyewitness accounts, phone records, and Greg's car's computer data. Their testimony, while not without its own antagonism with jurors, ostensibly helps Greg win a neutral ruling (of excusable death), though that still leaves him open to a lawsuit from the victim's family. In the final scene, Greg walks through a cadre of media outside the courtroom, and hears all of his antagonists making self-serving comments to the press. Thus, the heroic criminalist, who arguably saved another man's life in the incident, and was nearly killed in the process, is pitted against mediated cries for justice and thinly-veiled political posturing.[16]

In similar fashion, several other episodes show the criminalists in the courtroom, facing down hostile defense attorneys and skeptical judges. In these episodes, another one of Cole and Dioso-Villa's *CSI Effects* is arguably put forward, as our sympathies reside with the protagonists (i.e., the prosecution) rather than the defendants. We have witnessed their previous actions, and know them to be credible. Conversely, the series typically shows lawyers and even judges to be

Public justice: Greg faces the media after the mixed findings of the coroner's inquest which ruled the death of Demetrius James "excusable," in 7.7 "Post Mortem."

less than ethical, defending guilty clients in the interrogation room and casting doubt on the team's abilities in the courtroom. Indeed, the series' first two extensively represented judges were revealed to be a corrupt gambler and a serial killer, respectively. Lawyers are often shown to be arrogant but dim, as with the cocksure young attorney in 2.21, to whom Grissom remarks "I know the law, too, and I've actually been in a courtroom."[17] The attempted courtroom destruction of the entire team's credibility as forensic scientists in 3.2 is the most significant example of this type of plot, as it presents events from past episodes (i.e., first witnessed by viewers) in order to undermine the team's credibility. Moments that we experienced as character-building challenges are reinterpreted by the Hollywood star's defense team, under the guidance of Grissom's former mentor, as evidence of incompetence and possible corruption. Similarly, in 4.7, the team rallies to rebuild a rape-murder case in 24 hours after some evidence is found inadmissible (luckily so as well, because, in a rare instance of an acknowledged error by the team, the original defendant is actually innocent).

Forensic science on trial: Warrick is cross-examined about a knife found in a defendant's car, in 4.7 "Invisible Evidence."

End of Shift

The mediated discourses and anxieties surrounding alleged *CSI* Effects are, in the end, more culturally significant than the ambiguous claims about its influence in courtrooms. In the breathless claims and furrowed brows of prosecutors, a fictional television show is attributed with the power to change the way viewers, that is, citizens, regard standards of evidence, and hence the whole premise of criminal justice. The nexus of science, law, and popular culture may indeed be series like *CSI*, which not only generate compelling drama and dazzling spectacles, but also make conspicuous claims to reality, and expand outward throughout the culture due to their continued commercial successes. Accordingly, the *CSI* brand itself is ultimately the primary effect worth considering. As Michael Mopas argues, citing Bruno Latour's Actor-Network Theory, whether or not *CSI* is "real" is beside the point; hybridity is the default state of everything in our culture, and we should better understand how discourses about forensic science and *CSI* interact and reinforce each other, rather than only presume the series' representations are destructive.

Conclusion

> *Part of being a CSI is learning to work in the absence of absolute certainty. Each and every case brings us a new opportunity to learn something.* (Gil Grissom, 7.3 "Toe Tags")[1]

This book has argued for the continued vitality of a particular form of popular culture: mass-audience scripted narrative television. *CSI* has, in many ways, continued a function that has been performed in the past by series such as *Dragnet* (NBC, 1951–9), *Bonanza* (NBC 1959–73), *All In The Family* (CBS, 1971–9), *The Cosby Show* (NBC, 1984–92), and *ER* (NBC, 1994–2009): offering compelling and influential television storytelling regularly viewed by tens of millions of people. Like these others, *CSI* drew from established and familiar genres, narrative formats, and production styles, but also combined them into a fresh, engaging package that stood out from the rest of the prime-time schedule and commanded industrial, critical, and cultural attention.

However, as the calendar turns to the second decade of the twenty-first century, it is far from certain that the 60-year-old cultural form of mass-audience popular narrative television is still valid, at least in the United States. Broadcast network television, propelled by the expansion of diverse programming options across several media platforms, is finally succumbing to the logic of niche marketing, whereby potential audiences are aggregated in smaller numbers, and no individual series can stake a claim to any notion of a "cultural center." As recently as the early 2000s it was still common for regular episodes of prime-time entertainment series to be among the most viewed television events of any given year, virtually the only telecasts that now generate same audiences over 20 million or so today (i.e., roughly 6% of the total American television audience) are major sporting events and awards shows. Television *per se*, however experienced, is becoming even more integrated into everyday American life, but as its offerings are geared towards particular interests, the impact of individual television programs is shrinking.

This is not to say that contemporary US television programming has "failed" because of its fragmented viewership; far from it. The best programs in recent years have certainly offered significant, rewarding, and often challenging viewing, extending the medium's range of expressive possibilities. They deserve their accolades, scholarly interest, and devoted followings. Moreover, many of these series may have had small audiences (in the low millions) on cable networks like AMC, FX, HBO, SyFy, or Showtime, but have still registered in mainstream culture by virtue of those audiences' relatively privileged position in the cultural economy. In other words, one may not have actually watched AMC's *Mad Men*, but one most likely would know something about it due to its broad media coverage. The key point is that, as it is with every other cultural form, the economy of television is changing, and the old mass audience standard (e.g., garnering upwards of a quarter of the broadcast audience on any given night) is no longer viable or necessary. There are now many ways for a television series to successfully engage with audiences.

Where does that then leave *CSI*, and its legacy? In this era of narrow niches, *CSI* (along with most of the CBS "crime time" schedule) has clearly aspired to *broad*casting. The series and its offspring are meant to be "big-ticket" popular television, and not hidden gems tucked away on a small cable network. However, to their credit, the producers, cast and crew of *CSI* have delivered "mainstream" television without trying to formulate an archaic "mainstream" sensibility: that is, without wavering from difficult subject matter, complex aesthetics, and, in a decade otherwise dominated by dogma and suspicion, a refreshingly brazen ideology of diversity and intellectual curiosity (i.e., the CSI team, and particularly Grissom, do not tolerate bigots or fools gladly). It has presented a world not unlike television itself, where the production of visibility connects with both science and emotion, and generates narrative possibilities. It has cracked open the relationships between crime, investigation, and justice in twenty-first century America, and has explored the lives of those who must reconcile them, and find their own roles in the process. It has complicated the televisual presentation of place, offering a rich and diverse vision of one of the world's most iconic and singular cities. It has begged the question of society's relationship with television, justifiably claiming the mantles of both "entertainment" and "education" and complicating normative assumptions about the effects of popular culture. It is a text rich in concepts, meanings, and moments that this book could only begin to explore.

CSI is classic American television. It is significant not only for its brazen, unapologetic showmanship or its characters' ethical travails, but also for its thoughtful exploration of the medium itself as a compelling storytelling platform. It operates from a seemingly familiar television premise (investigating crimes), but renders it with uncommon intelligence and style. In an era of diminishing returns for old-style popular television, *CSI*'s consistent industrial success, cultural influence, and aesthetic engagement are major achievements on a scale that may never come again.

Appendix
CSI Episode Guide, 2000–9

Note: In the interests of clarity, this guide has been limited to only title, airdate, writer, and director information. Several online resources have full credit listings; I recommend in particular the episode guides at TV.com (http://www.tv.com/csi/show/19/episode.html).

Season 1 (2000–1)

1.1 Pilot (October 6, 2000):
Writer: Anthony E. Zuiker
Director: Danny Cannon

1.2 Cool Change (October 13, 2000):
Writer: Anthony E. Zuiker
Director: Michael Watkins

1.3 Crate 'n Burial (October 20, 2000):
Writer: Ann Donahue
Director: Danny Cannon

1.4 Pledging Mr. Johnson (October 27, 2000):
Writers: Josh Berman and Anthony E. Zuiker
Director: R. J. Lewis

1.5 Friends and Lovers (November 3, 2000):
Writer: Andrew Lipsitz
Director: Lou Antonio

1.6 Who Are You? (November 10, 2000):
Writers: Carol Mendelsohn and Josh Berman
Director: Danny Cannon

1.7 Blood Drops (November 17, 2000):
Writer: Ann Donahue
Director: Kenneth Fink

1.8 Anonymous (November 24, 2000):
Writers: Eli Talbert and Anthony E. Zuiker
Director: Danny Cannon

1.9 Unfriendly Skies (December 8, 2000):
Writers: Andrew Lipsitz, Carol Mendelsohn, and Anthony E. Zuiker
Director: Michael Shapiro

1.10 Sex, Lies, and Larvae (December 22, 2000):
Writers: Josh Berman and Ann Donahue
Director: Thomas J. Wright

1.11 I-15 Murders (January 12, 2001):
Writer: Carol Mendelsohn
Director: Oz Scott

1.12 Fahrenheit 932 (February 1, 2001):
Writer: Jacqueline Zambrano
Director: Danny Cannon

1.13 Boom (February 8, 2001):
Writers: Josh Berman, Ann Donahue, and Carol Mendelsohn
Director: Kenneth Fink

1.14 To Halve and to Hold (February 15, 2001):
Writers: Andrew Lipsitz and Ann Donahue
Director: Lou Antonio

1.15 Table Stakes (February 22, 2001):
Writers: Anthony E. Zuiker and Carol Mendelsohn
Director: Danny Cannon

1.16 Too Tough to Die (March 1, 2001):
Writer: Elizabeth Devine
Director: Richard J. Lewis

1.17 Face Lift (March 8, 2001):
Writer: Josh Berman
Director: Lou Antonio

1.18 $35 K O.B.O. (March 29, 2001):
Writer: Eli Talbert
Director: Roy H. Wagner

1.19 Gentle, Gentle (April 12, 2001):
Writer: Ann Donahue
Director: Danny Cannon

1.20 Sounds of Silence (April 19, 2001):
Writers: Josh Berman and Andrew Lipsitz
Director: Peter Markle

1.21 Justice is Served (April 26, 2001):
Writer: Jerry Stahl
Director: Thomas J. Wright

1.22 Evaluation Day (May 10, 2001):
Writer: Anthony E. Zuiker
Director: Kenneth Fink

1.23 Strip Strangler (May 17, 2001):
Writer: Ann Donahue
Director: Danny Cannon

Season 2 (2001–2)

2.1 Burked (September 27, 2001):
Writers: Anthony E. Zuiker and Carol Mendelsohn
Director: Danny Cannon

2.2 Chaos Theory (October 4, 2001):
Writers: Josh Berman and Eli Talbert
Director: Kenneth Fink

2.3 Overload (October 11, 2001):
Writer: Josh Berman
Director: Richard J. Lewis

2.4 Bully for You (October 18, 2001):
Writer: Ann Donahue
Director: Thomas J. Wright

2.5 Scuba Doobie-Doo (October 25, 2001):
Writers: Elizabeth Devine and Andrew Lipsitz
Director: Jefery Levy

2.6 Alter Boys (November 1, 2001):
Writer: Ann Donahue
Director: Danny Cannon

2.7 Caged (November 8, 2001):
Writers: Elizabeth Devine and Carol Mendelsohn
Director: Richard J. Lewis

2.8 Slaves of Las Vegas (November 15, 2001):
Writer: Jerry Stahl
Director: Peter Markle

2.9 And Then There Were None (November 22, 2001):
Writers: Eli Talbert, Josh Berman, and Carol Mendelsohn
Director: Richard J. Lewis

2.10 Ellie (December 6, 2001):
Writer: Anthony E. Zuiker
Director: Charlie Correll

2.11 Organ Grinder (December 13, 2001):
Writers: Elizabeth Devine and Ann Donahue
Director: Allison Liddi

2.12 You've Got Male (December 20, 2001):
Writers: Marc Dube and Corey Miller
Director: Charlie Correll

2.13 Identity Crisis (January 17, 2002):
Writers: Ann Donahue and Anthony E. Zuiker
Director: Kenneth Fink

2.14 The Finger (January 31, 2002):
Writers: Danny Cannon and Carol Mendelsohn
Director: Richard J. Lewis

2.15 Burden of Proof (February 7, 2002):
Writer: Ann Donahue
Director: Kenneth Fink

2.16 Primum Non Nocere (February 28, 2002):
Writer: Andrew Lipsitz
Director: Danny Cannon

2.17 Felonious Monk (March 7, 2002):
Writer: Jerry Stahl
Director: Kenneth Fink

2.18 Chasing the Bus (March 28, 2002):
Writer: Eli Talbert
Director: Richard J. Lewis

2.19 Stalker (April 4, 2002):
Writers: Danny Cannon and Anthony E. Zuiker
Director: Peter Markle

2.20 Cats in the Cradle (April 25, 2002):
Writer: Kris Dobkin
Director: Richard J. Lewis

2.21 Anatomy of a Lye (May 2, 2002):
Writers: Josh Berman and Andrew Lipsitz
Director: Kenneth Fink

2.22 Cross Jurisdictions (May 9, 2002):
Writers: Ann Donahue, Carol Mendelsohn, and Anthony E. Zuiker
Director: Danny Cannon

2.23 The Hunger Artist (May 16, 2002):
Writer: Jerry Stahl
Director: Richard J. Lewis

Season 3 (2002–3)

3.1 Revenge is Best Served Cold (September 26, 2002):
Writers: Anthony E. Zuiker and Carol Mendelsohn
Director: Danny Cannon

3.2 The Accused is Entitled (October 3, 2002):
Writers: Elizabeth Devine and Ann Donahue
Director: Kenneth Fink

3.3 Let the Seller Beware (October 10, 2002):
Writers: Carol Mendelsohn and Anthony E. Zuiker
Director: Danny Cannon

3.4 A Little Murder (October 17, 2002):
Writers: Naren Shankar and Ann Donahue
Director: Tucker Gates

3.5 Abra Cadaver (October 31, 2002):
Writers: Danny Cannon and Anthony E. Zuiker
Director: Danny Cannon

3.6 The Execution of Catherine Willows (November 7, 2002):
Writers: Elizabeth Devine and Carol Mendelsohn
Director: Kenneth Fink

3.7 Fight Night (November 14, 2002):
Writers: Andrew Lipsitz and Naren Shankar
Director: Richard J. Lewis

3.8 Snuff (November 21, 2002):
Writers: Bob Harris and Ann Donahue
Director: Kenneth Fink

3.9 Blood Lust (December 5, 2002):
Writers: Josh Berman and Carol Mendelsohn
Director: Charlie Correll

3.10 High and Low (December 12, 2002):
Writers: Naren Shankar and Eli Talbert
Director: Richard J. Lewis

3.11 Recipe for Murder (January 9, 2003):
Writers: Ann Donahue and Anthony E. Zuiker
Directors: Richard J. Lewis and J. Miller Tobin

3.12 Got Murder? (January 16, 2003):
Writer: Sarah Goldfinger
Director: Kenneth Fink

3.13 Random Acts of Violence (January 30, 2003):
Writers: Danny Cannon and Naren Shankar
Director: Danny Cannon

3.14 One Hit Wonder (February 6, 2003):
Writer: Corey Miller
Director: Feliz Enriquez Alcalá

3.15 Lady Heather's Box (February 13, 2003):
Writers: Josh Berman, Ann Donahue, Bob Harris, Andrew Lipsitz, Carol Mendelsohn, Naren Shankar, Eli Talbert, and Anthony E. Zuiker
Director: Richard J. Lewis

3.16 Lucky Strike (February 20, 2003):
Writers: Eli Talbert and Anthony E. Zuiker
Director: Kenneth Fink

3.17 Crash and Burn (March 13, 2003):
Writer: Josh Berman
Director: Richard J. Lewis

3.18 Precious Metal (April 3, 2003):
Writers: Andrew Lipsitz and Naren Shankar
Director: Deran Sarafian

3.19 A Night at the Movies (April 10, 2003):
Writers: Danny Cannon, Carol Mendelsohn, and Anthony E. Zuiker
Director: Matt Earl Beesley

3.20 Last Laugh (April 24, 2003):
Writers: Carol Mendelsohn, Bob Harris, and Anthony E. Zuiker
Director: Richard J. Lewis

3.21 Forever (May 1, 2003):
Writer: Sarah Goldfinger
Director: David Grossman

3.22 Play with Fire (May 8, 2003):
Writers: Andrew Lipsitz and Naren Shankar
Director: Kenneth Fink

3.23 Inside the Box (May 15, 2003):
Writers: Carol Mendelsohn and Anthony E. Zuiker
Director: Kenneth Fink

Season 4 (2003–4)

4.1 Assume Nothing (September 25, 2003):
Writers: Danny Cannon and Anthony E. Zuiker
Director: Richard J. Lewis

4.2 All for Our Country (October 2, 2003):
Writers: Richard Catalani, Andrew Lipsitz, and Carol Mendelsohn
Director: Richard J. Lewis

4.3 Homebodies (October 9, 2003):
Writers: Sarah Goldfinger and Naren Shankar
Director: Kenneth Fink

4.4 Feeling the Heat (October 23, 2003):
Writers: Eli Talbert and Anthony E. Zuiker
Director: Kenneth Fink

4.5 Fur and Loathing (October 30, 2003):
Writer: Jerry Stahl
Director: Richard J. Lewis

4.6 Jackpot (November 6, 2003):
Writers: Carol Mendelsohn and Naren Shankar
Director: Danny Cannon

4.7 Invisible Evidence (November 13, 2003):
Writer: Josh Berman
Director: Danny Cannon

4.8 After the Show (November 20, 2003):
Writers: Elizabeth Devine and Andrew Lipsitz
Director: Kenneth Fink

4.9 Grissom versus the Volcano (December 11, 2003):
Writers: Josh Berman, Carol Mendelsohn, and Anthony E. Zuiker
Director: Richard J. Lewis

4.10 Coming of Rage (December 18, 2003):
Writers: Richard Catalani and Sarah Goldfinger
Director: Nelson McCormick

4.11 Eleven Angry Jurors (January 8, 2004):
Writers: Josh Berman and Andrew Lipsitz
Director: Matt Earl Beesley

4.12 Butterflied (January 15, 2004):
Writer: David Rambo
Director: Richard J. Lewis

4.13 Suckers (February 5, 2004):
Writers: Josh Berman and Danny Cannon
Director: Danny Cannon

4.14 Paper or Plastic (February 12, 2004):
Writer: Naren Shankar
Director: Kenneth Fink

4.15 Early Rollout (February 19, 2004):
Writers: Elizabeth Devine, Carol Mendelsohn, and Anthony E. Zuiker
Director: Duane Clark

4.16 Getting Off (February 26, 2004):
Writer: Jerry Stahl
Director: Kenneth Fink

4.17 XX (March 11, 2004):
Writer: Ethlie Ann Vare
Director: Deran Sarafian

4.18 Bad to the Bone (April 1, 2004):
Writer: Eli Talbert
Director: David Grossman

4.19 Bad Words (April 15, 2004):
Writer: Sarah Goldfinger
Director: Rob Bailey

4.20 Dead Ringer (April 29, 2004):
Writer: Elizabeth Devine
Director: Kenneth Fink

4.21 Turn of the Screws (May 6, 2004):
Writers: Josh Berman, Richard Catalani, and Carol Mendelsohn
Director: Deran Sarafian

4.22 No More Bets (May 13, 2004):
Writers: Dustin Lee Abraham, Andrew Lipsitz, Judith McCreary, Carol Mendelsohn, and Naren Shankar
Director: Richard J. Lewis

4.23 Bloodlines (May 20, 2004):
Writers: Sarah Goldfinger, Carol Mendelsohn, Naren Shankar, and Eli Talbert
Director: Kenneth Fink

Season 5 (2004–5)

5.1 Viva Las Vegas (September 23, 2004):
Writers: Danny Cannon and Carol Mendelsohn
Director: Danny Cannon

5.2 Down the Drain (October 7, 2004):
Writer: Naren Shankar
Director: Kenneth Fink

5.3 Harvest (October 14, 2004):
Writer: Judith McCreary
Director: David Grossman

5.4 Crow's Feet (October 21, 2004):
Writer: Josh Berman
Director: Richard J. Lewis

5.5 Swap Meet (October 28, 2004):
Writers: David Rambo, Naren Shankar, and Carol Mendelsohn
Director: Danny Cannon

5.6 What's Eating Gilbert Grissom? (November 4, 2004):
Writer: Sarah Goldfinger
Director: Kenneth Fink

5.7 Formalities (November 11, 2004):
Writers: Dustin Lee Abraham and Naren Shankar
Director: Bill Eagles

5.8 Ch-Ch-Changes (November 18, 2004):
Writer: Jerry Stahl
Director: Richard J. Lewis

5.9 Mea Culpa (November 25, 2004):
Writer: Josh Berman
Director: David Grossman

5.10 No Humans Involved (December 9, 2004):
Writer: Judith McCreary
Director: Rob Bailey

5.11 Who Shot Sherlock? (January 6, 2005):
Writers: Richard Catalani and David Rambo
Director: Kenneth Fink

5.12 Snakes (January 13, 2005):
Writer: Dustin Lee Abraham
Director: Richard J. Lewis

5.13 Nesting Dolls (February 3, 2005):
Writer: Sarah Goldfinger
Director: Bill Eagles

5.14 Unbearable (February 10, 2005):
Writers: Josh Berman and Carol Mendelsohn
Director: Kenneth Fink

5.15 King Baby (February 17, 2005):
Writer: Jerry Stahl
Director: Richard J. Lewis

5.16 Big Middle (February 24, 2005):
Writers: Dustin Lee Abraham, Judith McCreary, and Naren Shankar
Director: Bill Eagles

5.17 Compulsion (March 10, 2005):
Writers: Josh Berman and Richard Catalani
Director: Duane Clark

5.18 Spark of Life (March 31, 2005):
Writer: Allen MacDonald
Director: Kenneth Fink

5.19 4 × 4 (April 14, 2005):
Writers: David Rambo, Sarah Goldfinger, Naren Shankar, and Dustin Lee Abraham
Director: Terrence O'Hara

5.20 Hollywood Brass (April 21, 2005):
Writers: Carol Mendelsohn and Sarah Goldfinger
Director: Bill Eagles

5.21 Committed (April 28, 2005):
Writers: Uttam Narsu, Sarah Goldfinger, and Richard J. Lewis
Director: Richard J. Lewis

5.22 Weeping Willows (May 5, 2005):
Writer: Areanne Lloyd
Director: Kenneth Fink

5.23 Iced (May 12, 2005):
Writer: Josh Berman
Director: Richard J. Lewis

5.24–25 Grave Danger (two parts): (May 19, 2005):
Writers: Carol Mendelsohn, Anthony E. Zuiker, and Naren Shankar
Director: Quentin Tarantino

Season 6 (2005–6)

6.1 Bodies in Motion (September 22, 2005):
Writer: Naren Shankar
Director: Richard J. Lewis

6.2 Room Service (September 29, 2005):
Writer: Henry Alonso Myers and Dustin Lee Abraham
Director: Kenneth Fink

6.3 Bite Me (October 6, 2005):
Writer: Josh Berman
Director: Jeffery Hunt

6.4 Shooting Stars (October 13, 2005):
Writer: Danny Cannon
Director: Danny Cannon

6.5 Gum Drops (October 20, 2005):
Writer: Sarah Goldfinger
Director: Richard J. Lewis

6.6 Secrets and Flies (November 3, 2005):
Writer: Josh Berman
Director: Terrence O'Hara

6.7 A Bullet Runs Through It (1) (November 10, 2005):
Writers: Carol Mendelsohn and Richard Catalani
Director: Danny Cannon

6.8 A Bullet Runs Through It (2) (November 17, 2005):
Writers: Richard Catalani and Carol Mendelsohn
Director: Kenneth Fink

6.9 Dog Eat Dog (November 24, 2005):
Writers: Dustin Lee Abraham and Allen MacDonald
Director: Duane Clark

6.10 Still Life (December 8, 2005):
Writer: David Rambo
Director: Richard J. Lewis

6.11 Werewolves (January 5, 2006):
Writer: Josh Berman
Director: Kenneth Fink

6.12 Daddy's Little Girl (January 19, 2006):
Writers: Henry Alonso Myers and Sarah Goldfinger
Director: Terrence O'Hara

6.13 Kiss-Kiss, Bye-Bye (January 26, 2006):
Writer: David Rambo
Director: Danny Cannon

6.14 Killer (February 2, 2006):
Writers: Dustin Lee Abraham and Naren Shankar
Director: Kenneth Fink

6.15 Pirates of the Third Reich (February 9, 2006):
Writer: Jerry Stahl
Director: Richard J. Lewis

6.16 Up in Smoke (March 2, 2006):
Writer: Josh Berman
Director: Duane Clark

6.17 I Like to Watch (March 9, 2006):
Writers: Richard Catalani and Henry Alonso Myers
Director: Kenneth Fink

6.18 The Unusual Suspect (March 30, 2006):
Writer: Allen MacDonald
Director: Alec Smight

6.19 Spellbound (April 6, 2006):
Writer: Jacqueline Hoyt
Director: Jeffrey Hunt

6.20 Poppin' Tags (April 13, 2006):
Writer: Dustin Lee Abraham
Director: Bryan Spicer

6.21 Rashomama (April 27, 2006):
Writer: Sarah Goldfinger
Director: Kenneth Fink

6.22 Time of Your Death (May 4, 2006):
Writers: David Rambo and Richard Catalani
Director: Dean White

6.23 Bang-Bang (May 11, 2006):
Writers: Anthony E. Zuiker and Naren Shankar
Director: Terrence O'Hara

6.24 Way to Go (May 18, 2006):
Writer: Jerry Stahl
Director: Kenneth Fink

Season 7 (2006–7)

7.1 Built to Kill (1) (September 21, 2006):
Writers: Naren Shankar and David Rambo
Director: Kenneth Fink

7.2 Built to Kill (2) (September 28, 2006):
Writers: Naren Shankar and Sarah Goldfinger
Director: Kenneth Fink

7.3 Toe Tags (October 5, 2006):
Writers: Richard Catalani and Douglas Petrie
Director: Jeffrey Hunt

7.4 Fannysmackin' (October 12, 2006):
Writer: Dustin Lee Abraham
Director: Richard J. Lewis

7.5 Double-Cross (October 19, 2006):
Writer: Marlane Gomard Meyer
Director: Michael Slovis

7.6 Burn Out (November 2, 2006):
Writer: Jacqueline Hoyt
Director: Alex Smight

7.7 Post Mortem (November 9, 2006):
Writers: Dustin Lee Abraham and David Rambo
Director: Richard J. Lewis

7.8 Happenstance (November 16, 2006):
Writer: Sarah Goldfinger
Director: Jean de Segonzac

7.9 Living Legend (November 23, 2006):
Writer: Douglas Petrie
Director: Martha Coolidge

7.10 Loco Motives (December 7, 2006):
Writer: Evan Dunsky
Director: Kenneth Fink

7.11 Leaving Las Vegas (January 4, 2007):
Writer: Allen MacDonald
Director: Richard J. Lewis

7.12 Sweet Jane (January 18, 2007):
Writers: Naren Shankar and Kenneth Fink
Director: Kenneth Fink

7.13 Redrum (January 25, 2007):
Writers: Carol Mendelsohn and Jacqueline Hoyt
Director: Martha Coolidge

7.14 Meet Market (February 1, 2007):
Writer: Dustin Lee Abraham
Director: Paris Barclay

7.15 Law of Gravity (February 8, 2007):
Writers: Richard Catalani and Carol Mendelsohn
Director: Richard J. Lewis

7.16 Monster in The Box (February 15, 2007):
Writers: Naren Shankar and Douglas Petrie
Director: Jeffrey Hunt

7.17 Fallen Idols (February 22, 2007):
Writer: Marlane Gomard Meyer
Director: Chris Leitch

7.18 Empty Eyes (March 29, 2007):
Writer: Allen MacDonald
Director: Michael Slovis

7.19 Big Shots (April 5, 2007):
Writer: Dustin Lee Abraham
Director: Jeff Woolnough

7.20 Lab Rats (April 12, 2007):
Writer: Sarah Goldfinger
Director: Brad Tanenbaum

7.21 Ending Happy (April 26, 2007):
Writer: Evan Dunsky
Director: Kenneth Fink

7.22 Leapin' Lizards (May 3, 2007):
Writer: David Rambo
Director: Richard J. Lewis

7.23 The Good, the Bad, and the Dominatrix (May 10, 2007):
Writer: Jacqueline Hoyt
Director: Alec Smight

7.24 Living Doll (May 17, 2007):
Writers: Naren Shankar and Sarah Goldfinger
Director: Kenneth Fink

Season 8 (2007–8)

8.1 Dead Doll (September 27, 2007):
Writers: Dustin Lee Abraham and Allen MacDonald
Director: Kenneth Fink

8.2 A La Cart (October 4, 2007):
Writer: Richard Catalani and Sarah Goldfinger
Director: Richard J. Lewis

8.3 Go to Hell (October 11, 2007):
Writer: Douglas Petrie
Director: Jeffrey Hunt

8.4 The Case of the Cross-Dressing Carp (October 18, 2007):
Writers: David Rambo and Jacqueline Hoyt
Director: Alec Smight

8.5 The Chick Chop Flick Shop (November 1, 2007):
Writer: Evan Dunsky
Director: Richard J. Lewis

8.6 Who and What (November 8, 2007):
Writers: Richard Catalani and Danny Cannon
Director: Kenneth Fink

8.7 Goodbye and Good Luck (November 15, 2007):
Writers: Allen MacDonald and Naren Shankar
Director: Kenneth Fink

8.8 You Kill Me (November 22, 2007):
Writers: Naren Shankar and Douglas Petrie
Director: Paris Barclay

8.9 Cockroaches (December 6, 2007):
Writer: Dustin Lee Abraham
Director: William Friedkin

8.10 Lying Down with Dogs (December 13, 2007):
Writers: Michael F.X. Daley and Christopher Barbour
Director: Michael Slovis

8.11 Bull (January 10, 2008):
Writer: David Rambo
Director: Richard J. Lewis

8.12 Grissom's Divine Comedy (April 3, 2008):
Writer: Jacqueline Hoyt
Director: Richard J. Lewis

8.13 A Thousand Days on Earth (April 10, 2008):
Writer: Evan Dunsky
Director: Kenneth Fink

8.14 Drops Out (April 24, 2008):
Writers: Dustin Lee Abraham and Allen MacDonald
Director: Jeffrey Hunt

8.15 The Theory of Everything (May 1, 2008):
Writers: Douglas Petrie and David Rambo
Director: Chris Leitch

8.16 Two and a Half Deaths (May 8, 2008):
Writers: Lee Aronsohn and Chuck Lorre
Director: Alec Smight

8.17 For Gedda (May 15, 2008):
Writers: Richard Catalani and Dustin Lee Abraham
Director: Kenneth Fink

Season 9 (2008–9)

9.1 For Warrick (October 9, 2008):
Writers: Allen MacDonald and Richard J. Lewis
Director: Richard J. Lewis

9.2 The Happy Place (October 16, 2008):
Writer: Sarah Goldfinger
Director: Nathan Hope

9.3 Art Imitates Life (October 23, 2008):
Writer: Evan Dunsky
Director: Kenneth Fink

9.4 Let It Bleed (October 30, 2008):
Writer: Corinne Marrinan
Director: Brad Tanenbaum

9.5 Leave Out All the Rest (November 6, 2008):
Writer: Jacqueline Hoyt
Director: Kenneth Fink

9.6 Say Uncle (November 13, 2008):
Writer: Dustin Lee Abraham
Director: Richard J. Lewis

9.7 Woulda, Coulda, Shoulda (November 20, 2008):
Writer: Allen MacDonald
Director: Brad Tanenbaum

9.8 Young Man with a Horn (December 4, 2008):
Writer: David Rambo
Director: Jeffrey Hunt

9.9 19 Down (December 11, 2008):
Writers: Carol Mendelsohn and Naren Shankar
Director: Kenneth Fink

9.10 One to Go (January 15, 2009):
Writers: Carol Mendelsohn and Naren Shankar
Director: Alec Smight

9.11 The Grave Shift (January 22, 2009):
Writers: Bradley Thompson and David Weddle
Director: Richard J. Lewis

9.12 Disarmed and Dangerous (January 29, 2009):
Writers: Evan Dunsky and Dustin Lee Abraham
Director: Kenneth Fink

9.13 Deep Fried and Minty Fresh (February 12, 2009):
Writers: Corinne Marrinan and Sarah Goldfinger
Director: Alec Smight

9.14 Miscarriage of Justice (February 19, 2009):
Writers: Jacqueline Hoyt and Richard Catalani
Director: Louis Shaw Milito

9.15 Kill Me If You Can (February 26, 2009):
Writers: David Weddle, Bradley Thompson and Allen MacDonald
Director: Nathan Hope

9.16 Turn, Turn, Turn (March 5, 2009):
Writer: Tom Mularz
Director: Richard J. Lewis

9.17 No Way Out (March 12, 2009):
Writer: Fuliva Charles-Lindsay
Director: Alec Smight

9.18 Mascara (April 2, 2009):
Writer: Dustin Lee Abraham
Director: William Friedkin

9.19 The Descent of Man (April 9, 2009):
Writer: Evan Dunsky
Director: Chris Leitch

9.20 A Space Oddity (April 16, 2009):
Writers: Bradley Thompson and David Weddle
Director: Michael Nankin

9.21 If I Had A Hammer . . . (April 23, 2009):
Writers: Corinne Marrinan and Allen MacDonald
Director: Brad Tanenbaum

9.22 The Gone Dead Train (April 30, 2009):
Writer: Jacqueline Hoyt
Director: Alec Smight

9.23 Hog Heaven (May 7, 2009):
Writer: David Rambo
Director: Louis Shaw Milito

9.24 All In (May 14, 2009):
Writers: Richard Catalani and Evan Dunsky
Director: Paris Barclay

Notes

Introduction: Why *CSI* Matters

1. Josh Berman, scriptwriter (hereafter scr(s).), "Overload," *CSI* 2.3, originally broadcast October 11, 2001.
2. However, the publication of Cohan's thoughtful analysis (in the *BFI Television Classics* series), as well as recent anthologies from I.B. Tauris and Lexington indicates that at least scholarly engagement with the series is now rising.
3. See Amanda D. Lotz (2007: 27–48.).
4. See, for example, Lisa Schwarzbaum, "TV Is King!" *Entertainment Weekly*, July 3, 2006, accessed on March 30, 2010 at: http://www.ew.com/ew/article/0,,1176435,00.html
5. Indeed, one of its stylistic (though not narrative) offshoots, *NCIS* (CBS, 2003–), is, as of this writing, the highest-rated scripted series on television in the 2009–10 season, and has itself generated a popular spinoff, *NCIS: Los Angeles* (CBS, 2009–).

Chapter 1: Science, Spectacle, and Storytelling

1. Elizabeth Devine and Carol Mendelsohn, scrs., "The Execution of Catherine Willows," *CSI* 3.6, originally broadcast November 7, 2002.
2. *Columbo* was technically a Los Angeles police detective, but rarely interacted directly with the department or any other detective or officer.
3. What I mean by the "dominant stylistic sensibility" is similar to Caldwell's argument about "excessive televisuality" in 1980s–90s TV. Most 2000s dramas, and particularly those with some cult and/or critical cachet, operate with a similar, self-conscious style that attempts to distinguish itself from "normal" television (however uncertain that concept is by now).

Thus, series as otherwise diverse as *Six Feet Under*, *Lost*, *House*, *Battlestar Galactica*, *The Wire*, *Desperate Housewives*, *Mad Men*, and all three *CSI*s, all share the same propensity towards self-aware, extra-normal stylization.
4   In 2004, *CSI* was even nominated for a Saturn Award, given to popular science fiction texts, not crime dramas.
5   Jerry Stahl, scr., "Fur and Loathing," *CSI* 4.5, originally broadcast October 30, 2003.
6   Although the team is almost always said to be working the "night shift," most episodes show them working their cases at both night and day.
7   This attractive representation of the work of investigation may have even inspired people to pursue careers in forensic science, as interest in the profession and its training courses surged in the early 2000s in the US and many of the countries where *CSI* was particularly popular. See chapter 4 for more on how these extra-textual "*CSI* effects" were generated both by the entire *CSI* franchise and its media coverage.
8   Sarah Goldfinger, scr., "Coming of Rage," *CSI* 4.10, originally broadcast December 18, 2003.

Chapter 2:   What Happens in *CSI*'s Vegas

1   Jerry Stahl, scr., "Slaves of Las Vegas," *CSI* 2.8, originally broadcast November 15, 2001.
2   Key historical Las Vegas accounts include Marc Cooper (2004); Sally Denton and Roger Morris (2001); Ed Reid and Ovid Demaris (1964); Hal Rothman (2003).
3   Las Vegas Convention and Visitors Authority, *Vegas FAQs 2008*, March 2009, accessed on March 30, 2010 at: http://lvcva.com/getfile/2008VegasFAQs.pdf
4   The actual slogan is "what happens here, stays here"; the substitution of "Vegas" is still the subject of a lengthy legal battle with an independent souvenir dealer.
5   Eli Talbert and Anthony Zuiker, scrs., "Lucky Strike," *CSI* 3.16, originally broadcast February 20, 2003.
6   Richard Catalani and David Rambo, scrs., "Time of Your Death," *CSI* 6.22, originally broadcast May 4, 2006.
7   In the same episode, Warrick finds himself under the thumb of a crooked judge, for whom he had been placing sports bets. Again, the allure of easy money is revealed to be a trap.

NOTES TO PAGES 42-58   131

8   Andrew Lipsitz and Ann Donahue, scrs., "To Halve and to Hold," *CSI* 1.14, originally broadcast February 15, 2001.
9   Danny Cannon and Anthony E. Zuiker, scrs., "Assume Nothing," *CSI* 4.1, originally broadcast September 25, 2003.
10 Catherine's background as an exotic dancer and Warrick's recovering gambling addiction, each tied to their Vegas upbringing, are both pounced upon by the defense lawyers.
11 As the seedy downtown hotel manager remarks upon the discovery of the body in one of his room's bathtubs, "that's hardly our first suicide." Danny Cannon and Carol Mendelsohn, scr., "Viva Las Vegas," *CSI* 5.1, originally broadcast September 23, 2004.
12 In a similar fashion, she is especially offended by insensitive parenting, and reserves her harshest judgments for parents who have either exploited or allowed their children into dangerous situations.
13 Judith McCreary, scr., "Harvest," *CSI* 5.3, originally broadcast October 4, 2004.
14 Jacqueline Zambrano, scr., "Fahrenheit 932," *CSI* 1.12, originally broadcast February 1, 2001.
15 Dustin Lee Abraham and Naren Shankar, scrs., "Formalities," *CSI* 5.7, originally broadcast November 11, 2004.
16 Dustin Lee Abraham, scr., "Fannysmackin'," *CSI* 7.4, originally broadcast October 12, 2006.
17 Carol Mendelsohn and Anthony Zuiker, scrs., "Table Stakes," *CSI* 1.15, originally broadcast February 22, 2001.
18 Douglas Petrie, scr., "Living Legend," *CSI* 7.9, originally broadcast November 23, 2006.
19 Eli Talbert and Anthony E. Zuiker, scrs., "Lucky Strike," *CSI* 3.16, originally broadcast February 20, 2003.

Chapter 3:   Finding Balance

1   Areanne Lloyd, scr., "Weeping Willows," *CSI* 5.22, originally broadcast May 5, 2005.
2   Medical dramas in particular are rife with such moments, as residents must prove their mettle under the judging gaze of attending physicians, nurses, and patients' families.
3   The original *Star Trek* and its first spin-off, *Star Trek: The Next Generation* functioned almost exclusively between these ostensible emotional poles, as starship captains Kirk and Picard mediated logic and passion in their duties.

4. Only Hodges, the lab technician, seems to struggle as well in this manner, though mostly because he openly aspires to be like Grissom.
5. While Holmes' morphine habit might be regarded in a similar manner, it is scarcely mentioned in the original Doyle stories, let alone made an issue.
6. Josh Berman, scr., "Face Lift," *CSI* 1.17, originally broadcast March 8, 2001.
7. Ann Donahue, scr., "Burden of Proof," *CSI* 2.15, originally broadcast February 7, 2002.
8. Josh Berman, Ann Donahue, Bob Harris, Andrew Lipsitz, Carol Mendelsohn, Naren Shankar, Eli Talbert, and Anthony E. Zuiker, scrs., "Lady Heather's Box," *CSI* 3.15, originally broadcast February 13, 2003.
9. David Rambo, scr., "Butterflied," *CSI* 4.12, originally broadcast January 15, 2004.
10. Anthony Zuiker, scr., "Ellie," *CSI* 2.10, originally broadcast December 6, 2001.
11. That said, producers and Petersen have indicated that he may return to the series in a guest-starring capacity at some point, though no plans have been announced at the time of this writing.
12. Josh Berman, scr., "Invisible Evidence," *CSI* 4.7, originally broadcast November 13, 2003.
13. Andrew Lipsitz and Elizabeth Devine, scrs., "After The Show," *CSI* 4.8, originally broadcast November 20, 2003.
14. Naren Shankar, scr., "Bodies in Motion," *CSI* 6.1, originally broadcast September 22, 2005.
15. Judith McCreary, scr., "No Humans Involved," *CSI* 5.10, originally broadcast December 9, 2004.
16. Elizabeth Devine, scr., "Too Tough To Die," *CSI* 1.16, originally broadcast March 1, 2001.
17. Evan Dunsky, scr., "The Chick Chop Flick Shop," *CSI* 8.5, originally broadcast November 1, 2007.
18. Allen MacDonald and Carol Mendelsohn, scrs., "Leaving Las Vegas," *CSI* 7.11, originally broadcast January 4, 2007.
19. Although Warrick was the only non-white regular character on the show until the arrival of Ray Langston (played by Laurence Wishburne) in season nine, several other non-white characters have appeared as LVPD personnel, including Detectives Chris Cavaliere (Jose Zuniga), Cyrus Lockwood (Jeffrey D. Sams), and Sam Vega (Geoffrey Rigas); lab technicians Mia Dickerson (Aisha Tyler), and Archie Johnson (Archie Kao); and coroner Jenna Williams (Judith Scott).

20 Richard J. Lewis, Allen MacDonald, and Carol Mendelsohn, scrs., "For Warrick," *CSI* 9.1, originally aired October 9, 2008.
21 Josh Berman and Andrew Lipsitz, scrs., "Eleven Angry Jurors," *CSI* 4.11, originally broadcast January 8, 2004.
22 Sarah Goldfinger, "Gum Drops," *CSI* 6.5, originally broadcast October 20, 2005.

Chapter 4: *CSI* Effects

1 Anthony E. Zuiker and Richard Catalani, scrs., "I Like to Watch," *CSI* 6.17, originally aired March 9, 2006.
2 Quoted in Abbie Bernstein (2007).
3 According to an analysis first published in the UK Radio Times in 2006, *CSI: Miami* was the top-rated program in the world in 2005, as it ranked in the most countries' top 10 most-watched series. "'CSI' Show Most Popular in the World," *BBC News*, July 31, 2006, accessed March 31, 2010 at: http://news.bbc.co.uk/2/hi/entertainment/5231334.stm
4 According to Nancy Tellem, then president of CBS Paramount Network Television Entertainment, "*CSI* was the last pilot we ordered and the last show that was scheduled." Quoted in Ray Richmond, "'CSI' 100th Episode: Scene of the Crime," *The Hollywood Reporter*, November 18, 2004, accessed March 31, 2010 at: http://www.hollywoodreporter.com/hr/search/article_display.jsp?vnu_content_id=1000723244
5 In particular, series creator Anthony Zuiker – a native Las Vegan, and former tram driver at the Mirage – benefited enormously from the series' success. *CSI* was his first major project of any stature, and its success led to a reported eight-figure development deal with CBS in 2003.
6 ABC's *Grey's Anatomy*, which debuted in early 2005, has met with some success against *CSI* (especially among 18–49 year old viewers), although *CSI* still generally prevails in the overall ratings.
7 Like the original *CSI*, however, *CSI: Miami* is mostly shot in southern California (Long Beach, specifically), with minimal production in south Florida.
8 *CSI* has crossed over with *CSI: Miami*, *CSI: NY*, and *Without a Trace*; *CSI: Miami* with *CSI: NY* (twice); and *CSI: NY* with *Cold Case*. In the second week of November 2009, a three-part crossover storyline was aired, tying together all three *CSI* series in one investigation.

9. Alex Navarro, "CSI: Hard Evidence Review," *Gamespot* (October 4, 2007) accessed 31 March 2010 at: http://www.gamespot.com/pc/adventure/csi4hardevidence/review.html
10. "About the Experience, Mission Statement," *CSI: The Experience*, accessed 31 March 2010 at: http://csitheexperience.org/about_mission.html
11. When I was on a jury selection panel in March 2009 in Dallas, I saw the prosecutor remind the potential jurors during voir dire that the real standards of guilt were different than those "seen on TV," that "beyond a reasonable doubt" does not necessarily mean absolute guilt.
12. Devine was involved with all three series at different points, 2000–7. Catalani only worked on the original series, as a consultant and writer, 2004–9.
13. Catalani does an almost identical overview of field kits in the season three set.
14. Anthony E. Zuiker and Richard Catalani, scrs. "I Like to Watch," *CSI* 6.17, originally aired March 9, 2006.
15. Douglas Petrie, scr., "Go to Hell," *CSI* 8.3, originally broadcast October 11, 2007.
16. In the ensuing settlement the family made with the LVPD, the family is awarded several million dollars. In the later episode "Big Shots" (7.19), reinforcing stereotypes of "undeserved" wealth, it is revealed that they purchased a lavish house and high-end consumer goods with the money. Demetrius' brother Aaron is apparently implicated in an unrelated crime, and Greg, still angry, struggles to keep his emotions towards him in check.
17. Josh Berman and Andrew Lipsitz, scrs., "Anatomy of a Lye," *CSI* 2.21, originally broadcast May 2, 2002.

Conclusion

1. Allen MacDonald, Carol Mendelsohn, Richard Catalani, and Douglas Petrie, scrs., "Toe Tags," *CSI* 7.3, originally broadcast October 5, 2006.

References

Bernstein, Abbie. 2007. "Naren Shankar." *CSI Magazine* 1:7, 38.
Caldwell, John T. 1995. *Televisuality: Style, Crisis, and Authority in American Television*. New Brunswick, NJ: Rutgers University Press.
Cavender, Gray and Deutsch, Sarah K. 2007. "CSI and Moral Authority: The Police and Science." *Crime Media Culture* 3.1: 67–81.
Cohan, Steven. 2008. *CSI: Crime Scene Investigation*. New York: Palgrave Macmillan.
Cole, Simon A., and Dioso-Villa, Rachel. 2007. "*CSI* and its Effects: Media, Juries, and the Burden of Proof." *New England Law Review* 41.3: 435–69.
Cooper, Marc. 2004. *The Last Honest Place in America: Paradise and Perdition in the New Las Vegas*. New York: Nation Books.
Debord, Guy (trans. Knabb, Ken). 1983. *The Society of the Spectacle*. London: Rebel Press.
Denton, Sally and Morris, Roger. 2001. *The Money and the Power: The Making of Las Vegas and Its Hold on America*. New York: Alfred A. Knopf.
Gever, Martha. 2005. "The Spectacle of Crime, Digitized: *CSI Crime Scene Investigation* and Social Anatomy." *European Journal of Cultural Studies* 8.4: 445–63.
Gray, Herman. 2004. *Watching Race: Television and the Struggle for Blackness*. Minneapolis: University of Minnesota Press.
Gray, Jonathan. 2010. *Show Sold Separately: Promos, Spoilers and Other Media Paratexts*. New York: New York University Press.
Hartley, John. 1999. *Uses of Television*. New York: Routledge.
Harrington, Ellen Burton. 2007. "Nation, Identity and the Fascination with Forensic Science in Sherlock Holmes and *CSI*." *International Journal of Cultural Studies* 10.3: 365–82.

Johnson, Victoria E. 2008. *Heartland TV: Prime Time Television and the Struggle for US Identity*. New York: New York University Press.

Lee, Susanna. 2004. "'These Are Our Stories': Trauma, Form and the Screen Phenomenon of *Law and Order*." *Discourse* 25.1 (Winter): 81–97.

Lotz, Amanda D. 2007. *The Television Will Be Revolutionized*. New York: New York University Press.

Lury, Karen. 2005. *Interpreting Television*. London: Hodder Arnold.

Mittell, Jason. 2004. *Genre and Television: From Cop Shows to Cartoons in American Culture*. New York: Routledge.

Mopas, Michael. 2007. "Examining the '*CSI* Effect' through an ANT Lens." *Crime Media Culture* 3.1: 110–17.

Postman, Neil. 1985. *Amusing Ourselves To Death: Public Discourse in the Age of Show Business*. New York: Penguin.

Rapping, Elayne. 2003. *Law and Justice As Seen On TV*. New York: New York University Press.

Reid, Ed and Demaris, Ovid. 1964. *The Green Felt Jungle*. New York: Pocket Books.

Roane, Kit. 2005. "The *CSI* Effect." *U.S. News & World Report* 138.15 (April 25): 48–54.

Rothman, Hal. 2003. *Neon Metropolis: How Las Vegas Started the Twenty-First Century*. New York: Routledge.

Scaggs, John. 2005. *Crime Fiction*. New York: Routledge.

Schweitzer, N.J. and Saks, Michael J. 2007. "The *CSI* Effect: Popular Fiction About Forensic Science Affects Public Expectations About Real Forensic Science." *Jurimetrics* 47 (Spring): 357–64.

Smith, Greg. 2007. *Beautiful TV: The Art and Argument of* Ally McBeal. Austin: University of Texas Press.

Thomas, Ronald R. 1999. *Detective Fiction and the Rise of Forensic Science*. New York: Cambridge University Press.

Toobin, Jeffrey. 2007. "The *CSI* Effect." *New Yorker* 83.11 (May 7): 30–35.

White, James. 2008. "The Music Man." *CSI Magazine* 4 (June/July): 76–80.

Index

"19 Down" (episode 9.9), 63

"Abra Cadaver" (episode 3.5), 22, 46, 65
"The Accused Is Entitled" (episode 3.2), 43, 63, 97, 100
Adams, Riley, 21, 71
"After the Show" (episode 4.8), 7, 19, 52, 67, 68
"A La Cart" (episode 8.2), 22
Alexander, Jason, 30
"All for Our Country" (episode 4.2), 16
Alliance Atlantis, 85
All in the Family, 102
Ally McBeal, 57
American Idol, 4, 24, 83
American Justice, 84
"Anatomy of a Lye" (episode 2.21), 24, 51, 58, 100
Armageddon (1998), 85
"Assume Nothing" (episode 4.1), 11, 42, 44, 63, 66, 76
audience demographics, 84, 103
autopsies, 17, 28, 31

"Bad to the Bone" (episode 4.18), 31, 52

Battlestar Galactica, 2, 3
Berman, David, 94
"Big Middle" (episode 5.16), 67
"Bite Me" (episode 6.3), 65
"Bloodlines" (episode 4.23), 47, 70
bodies, 17, 31
"Bodies in Motion" (episode 6.1), 16, 47, 67, 73
Bonanza, 102
"Boom" (episode 1.13), 74
Boston Legal, 56
Brass, Jim, 32–3, 48, 59, 75, 95
Braun, Sam, 47, 50–1, 66
Brown, Warrick, 7, 12, 20, 21, 26, 28, 42, 50, 54, 59, 64, 67, 68, 71–4, 76, 98, 99
Bruckheimer, Jerry, 8, 85–6
Buffy the Vampire Slayer, 5
"Built to Kill" (episodes 7.1, 7.2), 39, 47, 51, 65, 66
"A Bullet Runs through It" (episodes 6.7, 6.8), 24, 95
"Bully for You" (episode 2.4), 63
"Burden of Proof" (episode 2.15), 60, 74–5
"Burn Out" (episode 7.6), 33
"Butterflied" (episode 4.12), 26, 33, 62

INDEX

cable networks, 2
Caldwell, John, 15
Cannon, Danny, 8
Casino (1995), 37, 50
casinos, 38, 41, 45
Catalani, Richard, 9, 93
"Cats in the Cradle" (episode 2.20), 35
Cavender, Gray, 82
CBS, 82, 83, 84–6, 103
CGI, 5, 15, 17, 18
"Ch-Ch-Changes" (episode 5.8), 47
"Chaos Theory" (episode 2.2), 34
"Chasing the Bus" (episode 2.18), 28, 29, 70, 76, 78
"The Chick Chop Flick Shop" (episode 8.5), 71
children, 47–8, 65
Christie, Agatha, 34
cinema, 11
The Closer, 58
"Cockroaches" (episode 8.9), 72
Cohan, Steven, 2, 5, 19, 22, 47
Cold Case, 86
Cold Case Files, 84
Cole, Simon A., 90, 92, 99
Columbo, 12, 27, 59
comic books (*CSI*), 87
"Coming of Rage" (episode 4.10), 35
Con Air (1997), 85
"Cool Change" (episode 1.2), 42
Cooper, Marc, 46
The Cosby Show, 102
"Crash and Burn" (episode 3.17), 24, 33
"Crate 'n Burial" (episode 1.3), 73
crime, 9–10
crime drama (television), 12, 13–14, 15–16, 19, 32, 80, 84–5

crime fiction, 1, 9, 10–15, 24, 25, 34, 40
criminalist (as profession), 55–79, 84, 93
criminal justice system, 9, 12–13, 14, 34, 56, 80, 81, 89–92, 97, 99–101
Criminal Minds, 86
criticism, 1–4, 15, 80
"Cross Jurisdictions" (episode 2.22), 86
"Crow's Feet" (episode 5.4), 67
CSI Effect, 7, 80–101
CSI: The Experience (museum exhibit), 83, 88–9
CSI: Miami, 37, 83, 86
CSI: NY, 37, 83, 86
CSI shots, 19, 27
Curtis, Sofia, 59, 95

Dancing with the Stars, 24, 83
"Dead Doll" (episode 8.1), 52, 71
"Dead Ringer" (episode 4.20), 43
Debord, Guy, 15
detective fiction, *see* crime fiction
Deutsch, Sarah K., 82
Devine, Elizabeth, 9, 64, 93
Diagnosis Murder, 84
Dioso-Villa, Rachel, 90, 92, 99
DNA, 16, 19, 66, 76, 81, 82, 91
"Double-Cross" (episode 7.5), 72
Dourdan, Gary, 9, 12, 71, 73
"Down the Drain" (episode 5.2), 67, 68, 78
Dragnet, 12, 27, 36, 102
Dr. Quinn, Medicine Woman, 84
DVD, 4, 19, 93
DVR, 4

Eads, George, 9, 13, 74, 92
"Early Rollout" (episode 4.15), 72
Ecklie, Conrad, 63, 68, 98
"Eleven Angry Jurors" (episode 4.11), 75
"Ellie" (episode 2.10), 72
emotion, 58, 60, 61, 65, 70–1, 104
empathy, 74–6
"Empty Eyes" (episode 7.18), 71
"Ending Happy" (episode 7.21), 31
ER, 4, 56, 58, 102
"Evaluation Day" (episode 1.22), 73
evidence, 13–17, 22–3, 19–20, 27–35, 90–1
"The Execution of Catherine Willows" (episode 3.6), 8
exotic dancing, 21, 47, 64, 66–7

"Face Lift" (episode 1.17), 60
"Fahrenheit 932" (episode 1.12), 46, 48
"Family Affair" (episode 10.1), 20, 26
fandom, 59, 78–9
fan fiction, 78–9
"Fannysmackin'" (episode 7.4), 48, 78, 99
"Feeling the Heat" (episode 4.4), 31, 33, 65, 71, 97
"Felonious Monk" (episode 2.17), 21, 22, 64
"Fight Night" (episode 3.7), 20
film, 11, 12, 15, 25
fingerprints, 10, 19
Forensic Files, 84
forensic science, 10–11, 80, 81, 82, 83, 84, 87–8, 91, 92, 93–5, 101
"Forever" (episode 3.21), 32, 52
"For Gedda" (episode 8.17), 72, 73

"Formalities" (episode 5.7), 44, 48
"For Warrick" (episode 9.1), 63, 68, 74
Foucault, Michel, 9–10
Fox, Jorja, 9, 12, 69, 71
Fremont Street, 44–5, 47
The Fugitive, 85
"Fur and Loathing" (episode 4.5), 22, 27

gambling, 9, 17, 20, 21, 41, 44, 46, 72, 73
gender, 64–5, 66–7
Gever, Martha, 14, 16, 57
"The Good, the Bad, and the Dominatrix" (episode 7.23), 60
"Goodbye and Good Luck" (episode 8.7), 63, 71
"Go to Hell" (episode 8.3), 98
"Grave Danger" (episodes 5.24–25), 38, 52, 73, 75–6, 98
Gray, Herman, 73
Gray, Jonathan, 4
Grey's Anatomy, 24
Grissom, Gil, 1, 7, 12, 17, 35, 42, 43, 48, 49, 51, 53–4, 55, 59–63, 68, 72, 79, 100, 104
  and Catherine Willows, 47, 60, 65–6, 68
  and interrogation 33
  and Lady Heather, 60–1, 79
  and pedagogy, 16–17, 21–2, 74
  and Sara Sidle, 26, 61–2, 69–71, 79
  as scientist, 58, 98
  as supervisor, 68, 98
"Grissom's Divine Comedy" (episode 8.12), 97
Guilfoyle, Paul, 9
"Gum Drops" (episode 6.5), 54, 75, 76

The Hangover (2009), 37
"The Happy Place" (episode 9.2), 70
Harrington, Ellen Burton, 14
Hartley, John, 18
"Harvest" (episode 5.3), 16, 47
Hawaii Five-O, 36
Helgenberger, Marg, 9, 12, 64
Hill Street Blues, 37
Hitchcock, Alfred, 25
Hodges, David, 17, 28–9, 59, 95
Holmes, Sherlock, 12, 59
Homicide: Life on the Street, 3, 32, 56, 84

"I-15 Murders" (episode 1.11), 52, 69
"Identity Crisis" (episode 2.13), 33
"I Like to Watch" (episode 6.17), 26, 80, 95–6
"Inside the Box" (episode 3.23), 51, 52, 63
interrogation, 32–4
investigation, 1, 13–14, 15, 16, 23, 26–35, 84, 96
"Invisible Evidence" (episode 4.7), 13, 26, 64, 100–1

"Jackpot" (episode 4.6), 53–4
Johnson, Archie, 44
Johnson, Victoria, 84
journalism, 81
jury duty, 89–90
"Justice Is Served" (episode 1.21), 33, 60, 65

Keppler, Michael, 68–9
"Killer" (episode 6.14), 45
"Kiss-Kiss, Bye-Bye" (episode 6.13), 25, 49

"Lab Rats" (episode 7.20), 28–9
Lady Heather, 22, 60–1, 67
"Lady Heather's Box" (episode 3.15), 60–1, 64
Lake, Ronnie, 21, 98
Langston, Raymond, 21, 59
Las Vegas, 13
  children, 47–8
  as "everyday," 6, 39–40, 45–8
  Fremont Street, 44–5, 47
  history ("Old Vegas"), 6, 25, 40, 48–51
  as setting, 6, 36–54, 85
  shooting in, 38–9
  as "Sin City," 6, 21, 24–5, 39, 40–5, 47–8, 66
  Strip, 25, 38, 40, 41–2, 44, 45, 48
  as wilderness, 6, 40, 51–4
Las Vegas Convention and Visitors Authority, 41–2
law, *see* "justice system"
Law & Order, 27, 36, 57, 85
Law & Order: Special Victims Unit, 85
"Leapin' Lizards" (episode 7.22), 22
"Leave out All the Rest" (episode 9.5), 60
Leaving Las Vegas (1995), 37
"Leaving Las Vegas" (episode 7.11), 67
Lee, Susanna, 56
"A Little Murder" (episode 3.4), 65
"Living Doll" (episode 7.24), 33, 45, 52
"Living Legend" (episode 7.9), 50
logic, 58, 61, 65
Lost, 2, 3, 5, 78
Lost in America (1985), 37

"Lucky Strike" (episode 3.16), 31, 42, 51
Lury, Karen, 20
"Lying Down with Dogs" (episode 8.10), 52, 72

Mad Men, 2, 78, 103
"Mea Culpa" (episode 5.9), 98
Mendelsohn, Carol, 9, 64, 94
The Mentalist, 86
Miami Vice, 36
Miniature Killer, 45, 52, 63, 71
Mittell, Jason, 12
modernity, 10
Mojave Desert, 51–2
Mopas, Michael, 91, 101
Murder, She Wrote, 84
music, 25, 30
Muybridge, Eadweard, 11

narrative form, 14, 23–4
  episodic narrative, 23–8
  serial narrative, 7, 23, 55–79
Nash Bridges, 84
Navarro, Alex, 87–8
NCIS, 86
NCIS: Los Angeles, 86
"Nesting Dolls" (episode 5.13), 71
The New Detectives, 84
"No Humans Involved" (episode 5.10), 73, 78
"No More Bets" (episode 4.22), 21
novels (CSI), 87
Numb3rs, 86
NYPD Blue, 84

Ocean's 11 (1960), 37
"One to Go" (episode 9.10), 63, 71

"Organ Grinder" (episode 2.11), 21, 26, 77
"Overload" (episode 2.3), 1, 69

"Paper or Plastic" (episode 4.14), 38
paratext, 4
pedagogy, 17–18, 20–1, 28–9, 58, 81–2, 88
Petersen, William, 9, 12, 59, 63, 71
Phillips, David, 28, 31, 59, 94
photography, 10, 11, 28
"Pilot" (episode 1.1), 47
"Pirates of the Third Reich" (episode 6.15), 52, 60
"Play with Fire" (episode 3.22), 22, 61–2, 64, 78, 96
Poe, Edgar Allan, 10
police, 10, 12, 13, 26, 28, 30, 33, 43, 51, 64, 73, 75, 96–7
"popular television," 5–6, 23, 80, 102–3
Postman, Neil, 37
"Post Mortem" (episode 7.7), 21, 78, 99–100
"Precious Metal" (episode 3.18), 16, 22
"Primum Non Nocere" (episode 2.16), 61, 77
procedural drama, 55–6
production design, 30–2, 86
professionalism, 6, 7, 55–79
Promised Land, 84
Psycho (1960), 24

race, 72–3
radio drama, 12
"Random Acts of Violence" (episode 3.13), 73

Rapping, Elayne, 83, 90
"Rashomama" (episode 6.21), 26
ratings, 4, 83
realism, 18–20
reality television, 83–4, 85, 95
"Recipe for Murder" (episode 3.11), 22
"Redrum" (episode 7.13), 97
"Revenge Is Best Served Cold" (episode 3.1), 44
Roane, Kit, 91
Robbins, Albert "Doc," 17, 21, 31, 47, 58, 59, 63
The Rock (1996), 85
"Room Service" (episode 6.2), 25, 43, 44
Rothman, Hal, 42, 45–6

Saks, Michael J., 91
Sanders, Greg, 7, 12, 20, 21, 26, 48, 55, 59, 64, 68, 71, 72, 76–8, 79, 99
Saving Grace, 36
Scaggs, John, 10, 13
science, 9, 10–11, 13–14, 20, 21, 27–8, 58, 64, 81–2, 89, 93, 98, 101, 104
Schweitzer, N. J., 91
"Scuba Doobie-Doo" (episode 2.5), 58, 61
"Secrets and Flies" (episode 6.6), 65
Seinfeld, 85
setting, 6, 36–7, 80
sexuality, 22, 42, 60–1, 66–7, 79
Shankar, Naren, 9, 82
The Shield, 3, 36, 56
"Shooting Stars" (episode 6.4), 20, 22, 52

Sidle, Sara, 7, 12, 20, 21, 26, 28, 33, 35, 52, 58, 59, 61–2, 63, 67, 68, 69–71, 74, 76, 79, 98
Six Feet Under, 3
"Slaves of Las Vegas" (episode 2.8), 60–1, 67
Smith, Greg, 57
"Snakes" (episode 5.12), 22, 76
"Snuff" (episode 3.8), 29, 65
The Sopranos, 2, 3, 5, 78
"Sounds of Silence" (episode 1.20), 66
"Spark of Life" (episode 5.18), 26, 78
spectacle, 6, 9, 10–11, 15–17, 18–20, 82, 84, 89
"Stalker" (episode 2.19), 75
Star Trek, 19, 87
state power, 10, 12, 13, 43, 96–7
Stokes, Nick, 7, 13, 17, 21, 26, 33, 42, 54, 58, 59, 68, 71, 74–6, 95, 98, 99
"Suckers" (episode 4.13), 22
surveillance, 14, 28, 43–4
Survivor, 85
"Sweet Jane" (episode 7.12), 25, 68, 96
Szmanda, Eric, 9, 12, 76

"Table Stakes" (episode 1.15), 49
Tarantino, Quentin, 75
television drama, 2, 18, 23, 104
television industry, 84–7, 102–3
Thomas, Ronald R., 11, 14
"A Thousand Days on Earth" (episode 8.13), 65–6
"Time of Your Death" (episode 6.22), 42
"Toe Tags" (episode 7.3), 44, 102

"To Halve and To Hold" (episode 1.14), 42
"Too Tough to Die" (episode 1.16), 69, 70
Top Gun (1986), 85
Touched by an Angel, 84
tourists 37, 42, 48, 54
"Turn of the Screws" (episode 4.21), 65
Twin Peaks, 3

Ultimate CSI, 87, 94
"Unbearable" (episode 5.14), 51
"Unfriendly Skies" (episode 1.9), 35
"The Unusual Suspect" (episode 6.18), 71

video games, 83, 87–8
visibility, 5, 6, 11, 15–17, 19–20, 24, 25, 26–30, 44, 57
visual style, 1, 6, 18–20, 25, 30, 52, 80, 86
"Viva Las Vegas" (episode 5.1), 21, 25, 40, 42, 44–5, 70, 76, 77

Walker, Texas Ranger, 84
"Way to Go" (episode 6.24), 62

"Weeping Willows" (episode 5.22), 55, 66
Wellner, Jon, 94
"What's Eating Gilbert Grissom?" (episode 5.6), 33
The Who, 14, 50, 86
"Who Shot Sherlock" (episode 5.11), 78
Willows, Catherine, 7, 12, 21, 33, 50–1, 54, 55, 59, 63, 64–9, 71, 96, 98
and Gil Grissom 47, 60, 65–6, 68
and Sam Braun, 66
Willows, Lindsey, 47, 64, 66
The Wire, 2, 5, 36
Without a Trace, 86
Wynn, Steve, 40–1, 51

The X-Files, 84

"You Kill Me" (episode 8.8), 63
"Young Man with a Horn" (episode 9.8), 49
"You've Got Male" (episode 2.12), 51, 69

Zuiker, Anthony, 9, 84